# Basic
# Patterns
# in Union
# Contracts

### Twelfth Edition

D0874904

# Basic Patterns in Union Contracts

## Twelfth Edition

By the Editors of
*Collective Bargaining Negotiations & Contracts*

The Bureau of National Affairs, Inc., Washington, D.C. 20037

Published by BNA Books
1231 25th St., NW, Washington, D.C. 20037

Printed in the United States of America
International Standard Serial Number: 0521–8071
International Standard Book Number: 0–87179–638–4

⊛ ⟨GOU⟩ 302·l

# Contents

## 17
## Working Conditions: Safety and Health; Discrimination

# Introduction

This survey outlines the major types of provisions and their frequency in collective bargaining contracts. The purpose of the study is to provide negotiators with comparisons to their own agreements, bargaining proposals, and counterproposals. It further provides data on the most frequent means employed in handling bargaining issues and alternatives commonly used.

A file of over 3,000 agreements is maintained by The Bureau of National Affairs, Inc. These contracts are kept up to date with their latest renewals or amendments. From this file, a sample of 400 contracts is maintained with regard to a cross section of industries, unions, number of employees covered, and geographical areas.

The 400-contract sample forms the basis for analysis in this survey. In a majority of the provisions discussed and accompanying tables, the relative frequencies of particular practices are indicated separately for manufacturing and nonmanufacturing contracts. In addition, prevalent industry practices are noted.

For the first time, geographical analysis of contract provisions is included in the survey. A list of states included in each area follows:

*Middle Atlantic:* Delaware, District of Columbia, Maryland, New Jersey, New York, and Pennsylvania.

*Midwest:* Iowa, Kansas, Minnesota, Missouri, Nebraska, North Dakota, and South Dakota.

*New England:* Connecticut, Maine, Massachusetts, New Hampshire, Rhode Island, and Vermont.

*North Central:* Illinois, Indiana, Michigan, Ohio, and Wisconsin.

*Rocky Mountains:* Colorado, Idaho, Montana, and Wyoming.

*Southeast:* Alabama, Florida, Georgia, Kentucky, Louisiana, Mississippi, North Carolina, Puerto Rico, South Carolina, Tennessee, Virginia, and West Virginia.

*Southwest:* Arizona, Nevada, New Mexico, Oklahoma, Texas, and Utah.

*West Coast:* Alaska, California, Hawaii, Oregon, and Washington.

*Caution should be exercised* in the use of a sample analysis of this type:

(1) All frequency figures apply only to the contract sample studied. To the extent that the sample is broadly representative, these figures approximate general practice.

(2) There is some "turnover" in contracts making up the sample from year to year. Replacement of agreements generally is caused by company dissolution or union decertification. The representative

character of the sample is not significantly affected, however, by substitutions.

(3) More than one of the possible practices on any major bargaining issue may appear together in the same contract. Consequently, caution should be used in totalling different columns in the tabular presentation. Also, some percentages given for the frequency of various practices on the same subject do not total 100 percent because some contracts do not refer to the subject at all. In other cases, percentages do not total exactly 100 percent because of rounding to the nearest whole number.

(4) The presence of certain provisions in some contracts and their absence in others may be due to such different factors as varying industry conditions or merely the special emphasis given by company or union negotiators in the industries concerned.

(5) Caution also should be exercised in the comparison of figures in any current study with figures from a previous study. Sampling variations may introduce small percentage changes—either upwards or downwards—which do not reflect actual changes in contract practice. It is advisable, therefore, to avoid placing too great emphasis upon small percentage changes from one study to another. Larger changes more reliably connote changes in actual contract practice.

# 1

## Amendment and Duration

A majority (80 percent) of the contracts in this study have three-year terms, and 9 percent run for two years. Only five sample contracts run for one year or less. The number of contracts with a duration of four or more years increased—from 5 percent in 1986 to 9 percent, most of the shifts occurred in non-manufacturing industries.

Geographic analysis of the Basic Patterns database shows three-year agreements predominating in all regions, ranging from 54 percent in the Southwest area to 85 percent in the West Coast area.

*One-year agreements* make up 2 percent of the sample, compared to 3 percent in 1986 and 1 percent in 1983. Since the last survey the proportion of one-year contracts has dropped from 3 percent to 1 percent in the non-manufacturing sector and remained unchanged at 2 percent in manufacturing.

*Industry pattern:* Only seven of the 400 contracts surveyed have one-year terms. Six agreements are found in manufacturing: one each in electrical machinery, fabricated metals, foods, machinery, primary metals, and stone-clay-glass. In non-manufacturing, one construction agreement had a duration of one year.

*Two-year agreements* account for 9 percent of the sample, compared to 13 percent in the 1986 study and 17 percent in 1983. Two-year contracts appear with the same frequency in non-manufacturing and in manufacturing (9 percent).

*Industry pattern:* Sixty-five percent of the 26 industries in the study have at least one contract with a two-year duration. All petroleum contracts run for two years, continuing an industry tradition. In the paper industry, which is moving toward three-year agreements, only 7 percent of the contracts have two-year terms, down from 14 percent in 1986, 29 percent in 1983, and 43 percent in 1979.

*Three-year contracts* are found in 79 percent of contracts in manufacturing industries and 81 percent in non-manufacturing.

*Industry pattern:* All apparel, communications, leather, and maritime contracts in the sample have three-year terms. Other industries in which three-year contracts prevail are stone-clay-glass (92 percent), textiles and utilities (each 90 percent), retail (89 percent), transportation equipment (88 percent), and insurance and finance (86 percent).

1

# Length of Contract Term

*(Frequency Expressed as Percentage of Industry Contracts)*

| | Duration in Years* | | | |
|---|---|---|---|---|
| | 1 | 2 | 3 | 4 or more |
| ALL INDUSTRIES | 2 | 9 | 80 | 9 |
| MANUFACTURING | 2 | 9 | 79 | 9 |
| Apparel | — | — | 100 | — |
| Chemicals | — | 19 | 81 | — |
| Electrical Machinery | 5 | 10 | 80 | 5 |
| Fabricated Metals | 5 | 11 | 68 | 16 |
| Foods | 5 | 10 | 76 | 10 |
| Furniture | — | — | 83 | 17 |
| Leather | — | — | 100 | — |
| Lumber | — | — | 71 | 29 |
| Machinery | 4 | 12 | 81 | 4 |
| Paper | — | 7 | 79 | 14 |
| Petroleum | — | 100 | — | — |
| Primary Metals | 4 | 4 | 80 | 12 |
| Printing | — | — | 63 | 38 |
| Rubber | — | — | 83 | 17 |
| Stone-Clay-Glass | 8 | — | 92 | — |
| Textiles | — | 10 | 90 | — |
| Transportation Equipment | — | 3 | 88 | 9 |
| NON-MANUFACTURING | 1 | 9 | 81 | 10 |
| Communications | — | — | 100 | — |
| Construction | 3 | 21 | 69 | 7 |
| Insurance & Finance | — | 14 | 86 | — |
| Maritime | — | — | 100 | — |
| Mining | — | 8 | 58 | 33 |
| Retail | — | 4 | 89 | 7 |
| Services | — | 7 | 82 | 11 |
| Transportation | — | 8 | 76 | 16 |
| Utilities | — | 10 | 90 | — |

*Included in each yearly grouping are some contracts with durations of within six months of the specified year(s).

*Longer term agreements*—four years or more—make up 9 percent of the sample, compared to 5 percent in 1986. In manufacturing, agreements running four years or longer increased from 6 percent in 1986 to 9 percent in this survey; in non-manufacturing, they increased from 5 percent in 1986 to 10 percent.

*Industry pattern:* Of the 400 contracts, 37 have terms of four years or longer. Fifteen of those 37 agreements are found in the non-manufacturing sector—four each in mining and transportation, three in services, and two each in construction and retail. Twenty-two manufacturing agreements have longer terms—three each are in printing, primary metals, fabricated metals, and transportation equipment; two each in foods, lumber, and paper; and one each is found in electrical machinery, furniture, machinery, and rubber.

## Contract Reopeners

Reopening of a contract for amendment prior to its scheduled expiration date is called for in 11 percent of the sample, compared to 14 percent in the 1986 study. Reopener provisions appear more frequently in non-manufacturing (15 percent) than in manufacturing (8 percent) agreements.

Seventy-seven percent of these reopener provisions permit reopening for negotiation of wages, 23 percent for fringes, and 6 percent for cost-of-living adjustments. Forty-two percent of reopener provisions deal with other circumstances, most commonly changes in government regulations or enactment of legislation. In some cases, a single contract may be reopened for more than one reason.

### Reasons for Contract Reopenings

*(Frequency Expressed as Percentage of Contracts with Reopener Provisions)*

| Reopening Allowed | All Industries | Manufacturing | Non-manufacturing |
|---|---|---|---|
| For Wages | 77 | 75 | 79 |
| For Fringes | 23 | 22 | 24 |
| For Cost-of-Living Adjustments | 6 | 4 | 8 |
| Other | 42 | 44 | 40 |

All but one agreement with reopener provisions specify when the contract may be reopened. Of these, 13 percent allow for reopening at any time, 4 percent permit reopening annually, and 83 percent specify a set date or period of time.

Forty-nine percent of sample contracts with reopener provisions discuss the possibility of an impasse in reopener talks. Of the impasse provisions, 74 percent permit strikes and/or lockouts, 8 percent provide for cancellation or suspension of the agreement, and 17 percent call for arbitration. The option to strike and/or lock out appears more frequently in impasse clauses in manufacturing (82 percent) than in non-manufacturing (62 percent) industries. Impasse provisions calling for cancellation or suspension are equally common in non-manufacturing and manufacturing agreements (each with 8 percent), while those calling for arbitration are more frequent in non-manufacturing (17 percent) than in manufacturing (9 percent) contracts.

*Industry pattern:* Reopener provisions are found in agreements in 10 of the 17 manufacturing industries and in eight of the nine non-manufacturing industries. They appear in a majority of contracts in only two industries—textiles (60 percent) and leather (50 percent)—and are contained in 33 percent or less of contracts in the remaining industries.

## Contract Renewal _____

Most agreements provide for extension past their expiration date unless action is taken to amend or terminate. Automatic renewal provisions are found in 84 percent of agreements in the sample. Eighty-six percent of contracts providing for automatic renewal specify annual renewals. One percent specify renewal for three-year periods, and 13 percent specify renewal for indefinite periods. Renewal clauses occur with about the same frequency in manufacturing agreements as in non-manufacturing contracts.

*Industry pattern:* At least one-half of contracts in all industries provide for automatic renewal, most often with annual extensions. Renewal for an indefinite period is most common in petroleum (86 percent) and primary metals (36 percent).

Of agreements analyzed, 92 percent require explicit notice of a party's desire to terminate or amend the contract. This requirement is found with nearly the same frequency in manufacturing (92 percent) as in non-manufacturing (91 percent) agreements. Sixteen percent of notice requirements specify that proposed changes accompany the notice, and 29 percent specify when negotiations must begin.

Clauses requiring notice of a desire to amend or terminate are prevalent in all industries. A requirement that proposed changes accompany such notice appears in from 38 to 44 percent of stone-clay-glass, utilities and chemicals contracts.

A clause specifying when negotiations must begin appears in all rubber contracts and in at least one-half of all agreements in three industries—primary metals (52 percent), leather and transportation equipment (each 50 percent).

## Renegotiation of Contract _____

A minority (22 percent) of contracts make explicit provision for the status of the agreement when renewal negotiations extend beyond the expiration date. Such provisions are more common in manufacturing (26 percent) than in non-manufacturing (16 percent) contracts. Of these provisions, 44 percent call for extension only by mutual agreement, 28 percent call for automatic extension for a specified period with further extensions only by mutual agreement, and 27 percent call for automatic extension.

Eighteen percent of contracts included in this survey discuss problems arising from stalemated talks during negotiations. Of these, 49 percent specify that strikes and/or lockouts may be permitted, 45 percent state that the agreement may be terminated either automatically or by one of the parties, and 6 percent call for arbitration (either mandatory or by mutual consent).

# Amendment and Duration Provisions

*(Frequency Expressed as Percentage of Contracts in Each Region)*

| | All Regions | Middle Atlantic | Midwest | New England | North Central | Rocky Mountain | Southeast | Southwest | West Coast | Multiregion |
|---|---|---|---|---|---|---|---|---|---|---|
| **Term of Contract\*** | | | | | | | | | | |
| One year | 2 | 2 | 8 | — | 2 | — | 2 | 8 | — | — |
| Two years | 9 | 10 | 13 | 8 | 7 | 10 | 14 | 23 | 9 | 8 |
| Three years | 80 | 78 | 71 | 84 | 83 | 80 | 74 | 54 | 85 | 78 |
| Four or more years | 9 | 10 | 8 | 8 | 8 | 10 | 10 | 15 | 7 | 13 |
| Reopener Provisions | 12 | 7 | 8 | 4 | 6 | 10 | 24 | 31 | 11 | 20 |
| Separability Provision | 63 | 58 | 71 | 56 | 54 | 70 | 62 | 77 | 80 | 70 |
| Successorship Clause | 43 | 45 | 54 | 48 | 49 | 10 | 36 | 15 | 48 | 43 |

\* Included in each yearly grouping are some contracts with durations within six months of the specified year(s).

## Separability

The possibility that a portion of a contract may conflict with a state or federal law is considered in 63 percent of the sample contracts, unchanged from the 1986 study. Nearly one-half (49 percent) of these provisions simply state that the offending section shall be declared null and void without affecting other provisions. Thirty-eight percent of the clauses call for renegotiation of the matter; the remainder (14 percent) state that the illegal section shall be modified to conform with the law.

Separability provisions appear in 74 percent of non-manufacturing contracts, compared to 56 percent of manufacturing agreements. Under agreements containing separability provisions, renegotiation of illegal clauses is more prevalent in non-manufacturing (51 percent) than in manufacturing (27 percent); nullification is more prevalent in manufacturing (57 percent) than in non-manufacturing (38 percent); modification to conform with the law is more prevalent in manufacturing (16 percent) than in non-manufacturing (10 percent).

*Industry pattern:* Separability provisions are found in all industries and appear in at least half of the contracts in 18 of the 26 industries. Among those industries with the highest proportion of such provisions are: apparel, leather and petroleum agreements (each 100 percent); mining (92 percent), retail (89 percent), printing (88 percent), and construction (86 percent).

## Successorship Clause

Successorship clauses stipulate that any change in the management or identity of the parties to the contract shall not invalidate the agreement, but rather that the new management must assume the contractual obligations of the predecessor. These clauses appear in 43 percent of agreements included in this study, a climb from 38 percent in 1986 and 34 percent in 1983.

*Industry pattern:* Successorship clauses are more common in non-manufacturing (51 percent) than in manufacturing (38 percent) contracts. At least one-half of the contracts in eight industries contain such provisions: furniture (83 percent), communications (80 percent), transportation (76 percent), utilities (70 percent), apparel (67 percent), primary metals and retail (each 56 percent), and leather (50 percent).

# 2

# Discharge, Discipline, and Resignation

Discharge and discipline provisions are found in 97 percent of the 400 contracts analyzed. These clauses are included in all but one manufacturing agreement and excluded in only ten non-manufacturing contracts. Geographic analysis reveals that discharge-discipline provisions are contained in from 90 to 100 percent of agreements in areas designated in the Basic Patterns database.

## Grounds For Discharge

Grounds for discharge, found in 94 percent of sample contracts, are of two types—discharge for "cause" or "just cause" or discharge for specific offenses. Many contracts contain both "cause" or "just cause" and specific provisions.

"Cause" or "just cause" is stated as a reason for discharge in 86 percent of agreements studied—90 percent in manufacturing and 79 percent in non-manufacturing.

*Industry pattern:* Employees may be discharged for "cause" or "just cause" under all communications, furniture, leather, and machinery agreements and in at least 70 percent of contracts in all industries except construction, maritime, and printing.

**Specific grounds for discharge** are found in 75 percent of contracts in the database (82 percent in manufacturing and 65 percent in non-manufacturing). Grounds most frequently referred to in sample agreements are: violation of leave provisions, 37 percent; participation in unauthorized strikes, 34 percent; unauthorized absence, 30 percent; dishonesty or theft and violation of company rules, each 21 percent; intoxication, 20 percent; insubordination, 17 percent; incompetence or failure to meet standards, 16 percent; failure to obey safety rules, 14 percent; misconduct, 12 percent; and tardiness, 9 percent.

*Industry pattern:* Specific grounds for discharge are found in all leather, lumber, rubber, and textiles agreements and in at least 60 percent of contracts in all other industries except construction (31 percent), communications (30 percent), and petroleum (14 percent).

**Violation of leave** is mentioned as a reason for dismissal in 42 percent of manufacturing agreements and 28 percent of those in non-manufacturing. This cause for discharge appears in 75 percent of leather contracts, 63 percent of fabricated metals, 57 percent of insurance and finance, 56 percent of chemicals, and in 50 percent each of machinery, rubber, and textiles agreements.

**Unauthorized strike participation** is cause for discharge in 41 percent of manufacturing and in 24 percent of non-manufacturing agreements. Such provisions are found in 90 percent of textiles contracts, 67 percent of apparel, 62 percent of stone-clay-glass, 53 percent of transportation equipment, and in 50 percent each of leather, mining, and utilities agreements.

*Unauthorized absence* is cause for discharge in 38 percent of manufacturing agreements and in 17 percent of non-manufacturing contracts. Dismissals due to unauthorized absences are most common in rubber (67 percent), lumber (57 percent), and leather and furniture agreements (each 50 percent).

*Dishonesty or theft* is listed as a reason for discharge in 18 percent of manufacturing and 25 percent of non-manufacturing agreements. This cause for discharge appears most frequently in paper (57 percent), retail (52 percent), services (41 percent), and transportation (40 percent).

*Violation of company rules* is cause for dismissal in 24 percent of manufacturing agreements and in 16 percent of non-manufacturing contracts. It is specified in 57 percent of lumber contracts, 50 percent each of paper and printing, and in at least 30 percent of rubber (33 percent), chemicals (31 percent), and textiles (30 percent).

*Intoxication* may lead to discharge in 16 percent of manufacturing agreements and 26 percent of non-manufacturing agreements. Intoxication most frequently is specified as a reason for discharge in the following industries: paper (57 percent), maritime (50 percent), retail (48 percent), and services (41 percent).

*Insubordination* is a reason for dismissal in 16 percent of manufacturing contracts and 19 percent of non-manufacturing contracts. Discharge for insubordination is specified in 43 percent of paper, 38 percent of stone-clay-glass, and 30 percent each of retail, services, and textiles agreements.

*Incompetence or failure to meet standards* is cause for dismissal in 18 percent of manufacturing and 13 percent of non-manufacturing contracts. This reason for discharge is found in 50 percent of printing, 43 percent of paper, and in at least 30 percent of contracts in apparel, maritime, and stone-clay-glass.

*Failure to obey safety rules* is cause for discharge in 14 percent of manufacturing and 15 percent of non-manufacturing contracts. This reason for discharge appears in 36 percent of paper, 33 percent of mining, and 31 percent of stone-clay-glass agreements.

*Misconduct* is stated as cause for discharge in 12 percent each of manufacturing and non-manufacturing agreements. It is cause for dismissal in 38 percent of maritime, 33 percent of furniture, 29 percent each of paper and lumber, 25 percent of leather, and 20 percent of textiles contracts.

*Tardiness* is cause for discharge in 12 percent of manufacturing and 5 percent of non-manufacturing agreements. It is most often specified in agreements in leather (50 percent), lumber (29 percent), and electrical machinery (25 percent).

Often, causes for discharge listed above are sufficient grounds for immediate discharge. Many contracts, however, allow a number of offenses before an employee is terminated.

## Discharge Procedures

Procedures for discharge are found in 64 percent of contracts in the database. These clauses appear in 69 percent of manufacturing and 54 percent of non-manufacturing agreements. Provisions vary considerably and may require that the union be notified in advance of discharge or be present during discharge, that a predischarge hearing be held, or that a written notice be given to the employee, the union, or both.

### Discharge Procedures

*(Frequency Expressed as Percentage of Contracts)*

| | Notice | | | |
|---|---|---|---|---|
| | To Union (Before or During Discharge) | To Union (After Discharge) | To Employee or Union or Both in Writing | Hearings Before Discharge |
| All Industries | 28 | 26 | 40 | 19 |
| Manufacturing | 32 | 29 | 40 | 22 |
| Non-manufacturing | 21 | 23 | 40 | 14 |

**Predischarge hearings** are permitted under 19 percent of contracts surveyed (22 percent of manufacturing and 14 percent of non-manufacturing agreements). Under these provisions, an employee usually is suspended for a given number of days during which a hearing is to take place. Of agreements allowing predischarge hearings, 89 percent state that a union representative may be present.

*Industry pattern:* Predischarge hearings are most common in fabricated metals (53 percent), mining (50 percent), primary metals (48 percent), transportation (36 percent), and machinery (35 percent).

**Notice of discharge** is given to the union in advance of discharge or a union representative is present during the discharge proceedings under 28 percent of agreements—32 percent in manufacturing and 21 percent in non-manufacturing. Twenty-six percent of contracts (29 percent of manufacturing and 23 percent of non-manufacturing) require that notice be given to the union after discharge.

*Industry pattern:* Notice to the union (either before, during, or after discharge) is required most frequently in leather (100 percent), apparel (89 percent), rubber (83 percent), transportation equipment (79 percent), mining (75 percent), insurance and finance (71 percent), and is included in at least 60 percent of contracts in foods, textiles, machinery, communications, furniture, primary metals, and utilities.

*Written notice of discharge* is given to the employee, union, or both under 40 percent of agreements—40 percent each of manufacturing and non-manufacturing.

*Industry pattern:* This requirement most often appears in leather (75 percent), insurance and finance (71 percent), rubber (67 percent), printing (63 percent), services and apparel (each 56 percent), transportation equipment (53 percent), transportation (52 percent), and furniture (50 percent) agreements.

### Discharge Provisions

*(Frequency Expressed as Percentage of Contracts in Each Region)*

|  | Discharge for Cause | Specific Grounds for Discharge | Notice to Union of Discharge | Written Explanation of Discharge | Appeals from Discharge |
|---|---|---|---|---|---|
| All Regions | 86 | 75 | 54 | 40 | 76 |
| Middle Atlantic | 84 | 71 | 60 | 34 | 70 |
| Midwest | 96 | 67 | 58 | 42 | 67 |
| New England | 84 | 76 | 48 | 36 | 76 |
| North Central | 87 | 78 | 57 | 39 | 79 |
| Rocky Mountain | 70 | 60 | 30 | 40 | 40 |
| Southeast | 84 | 90 | 44 | 34 | 80 |
| Southwest | 85 | 77 | 23 | 39 | 85 |
| West Coast | 83 | 76 | 44 | 35 | 72 |
| Multiregion | 87 | 65 | 68 | 60 | 90 |

## Appeals Procedures

Discharge may be appealed under 76 percent of contracts studied—81 percent of manufacturing and 69 percent of non-manufacturing agreements. Many contracts specify a special time limit in which a discharge must be appealed.

*Industry pattern:* Provisions for appeals from discharge appear in all fabricated metals, communications, leather, petroleum, and rubber industry agreements and in at least 50 percent of contracts in all other industries except construction (28 percent).

*Special time limits* within which discharges must be appealed are imposed in 52 percent of contracts in the database. Under these provisions, the most common limits are 5 days (28 percent), 10 days (20 percent), 3 days (15 percent), 7 days (13 percent), 2 days (7 percent), and 15 days (6 percent).

## Appeals Procedures
*(Frequency Expressed as Number of Contracts)*

| | Time Limit in Days | | | | Reinstatement | |
|---|---|---|---|---|---|---|
| | 1-5 | 6-10 | 11-20 | Over 20 | Full Back Pay | Pay At Arbiter's Discretion |
| Discretion | | | | | | |
| All Industries | 108 | 70 | 22 | 6 | 73 | 69 |
| Manufacturing | 89 | 42 | 11 | 3 | 49 | 51 |
| Non-manufacturing | 19 | 28 | 11 | 3 | 24 | 18 |

## Reinstatement with Back Pay

Reinstatement with back pay for employees improperly discharged is required in 37 percent of sample contracts—42 percent of manufacturing and 29 percent of non-manufacturing agreements. Of these provisions, 49 percent grant full back pay, 46 percent leave the amount awarded to the arbiter's discretion, and 5 percent place a limitation on the amount awarded. In some instances unemployment compensation or money earned from other jobs may be deducted from back pay.

*Industry pattern:* Reinstatement with back pay is mentioned in all rubber agreements, in 78 percent of apparel, 75 percent of leather, 70 percent of utilities, and in at least 60 percent of contracts in furniture and textiles.

## Discipline Short of Discharge

Disciplinary measures short of discharge are contained in 77 percent of contracts analyzed. These provisions are found in 84 percent of manufacturing and 65 percent of non-manufacturing contracts.

Sixty-seven percent of contracts analyzed mention one or more of the following types of disciplinary measures—suspension, layoff, transfer, and demotion. Of these contracts, 94 percent refer to suspension, 22 percent to layoff, 8 percent to demotion, and 1 percent to transfer.

**Warning before disciplinary action** is called for in 40 percent of contracts in the database—42 percent in manufacturing and 36 percent in non-manufacturing. Of these clauses, 52 percent require that the employee be warned before disciplinary action is taken; 48 percent specify that the employee and union be warned.

*Industry pattern:* These provisions are found in 67 percent each of retail and rubber, 60 percent of textiles, and in at least half of contracts in services (56 percent), primary metals (52 percent), and leather and electrical machinery (each 50 percent).

**Notice to the union** before, during, or after disciplinary action is required in 50 percent of sample contracts—57 percent in manufacturing and 39 percent in non-manufacturing. Of these provisions, 59 percent require that the union either be notified in advance of discipline or be present during the disciplinary proceedings. The remainder require notice to the union after the fact.

*Industry pattern:* Notice to the union of disciplinary action is required by all rubber contracts, 75 percent in those in mining and leather, 72 percent in primary metals, 71 percent in transportation equipment, 70 percent in textiles, and in at least 60 percent of apparel and services (each 67 percent), fabricated metals (63 percent), and foods (62 percent).

*"Statute of limitations"* clauses, under which past offenses are removed from an employee's record after a specified period of time, appear in 36 percent of contracts analyzed. Limitations appear in 39 percent of manufacturing and 32 percent of non-manufacturing contracts.

*Industry pattern:* These clauses appear in 75 percent of leather agreements, 67 percent of those in rubber, 63 percent of services, 56 percent of primary metals, and 53 percent of transportation equipment.

## Resignation Procedures

Resignation procedures are found in only 8 percent of contracts in the database—4 percent in manufacturing and 14 percent in non-manufacturing agreements. All but one of the resignation procedures provisions require prior notification to the employer, and 47 percent impose a penalty for failure to give advance notice.

# 3

## Insurance

Insurance benefits are mentioned in most of the 400 contracts in CBNC's Basic Patterns database. Some contracts include fully detailed plans, others contain only statements or amendments referring to existing benefits, and still others merely stipulate the employer's contribution to an existing health and welfare plan.

The following analysis is based on 214 plans for which sufficient detail on insurance benefits was available.

A sharp rise over the last three years in the percentage of comprehensive medical care plans that replace basic hospitalization and surgical benefits and cover major medical expenses has caused a corresponding decline in the percentage of traditional plans providing these benefits. Thirty-seven percent of plans in this year's survey provide comprehensive medical coverage up from 21 percent in the 1986 study. Basic hospitalization benefits are provided in 63 percent of sample plans (down from 79 percent in the 1986 survey), surgical in 61 percent (down from 77 percent), and major medical in 57 percent (down from 74 percent).

The percentage of plans providing life insurance increased to 99 percent from 96 percent in the 1986 analysis; the percentage of plans providing sickness and accident (83 percent) and accidental death and dismemberment (74 percent) benefits was unchanged.

Since the 1986 study, there has been an increase in the number of plans providing coverage for dental and vision care and prescription drugs.

### Employee Insurance Coverage

*(Frequency Expressed as Percentage of Plans)*

|  | Life | AD&D | S&A | Hosp. | Surg. | Maj. Med. | Comp. Med. | Dent. |
|---|---|---|---|---|---|---|---|---|
| All Industries | 99 | 74 | 83 | 63 | 61 | 57 | 37 | 83 |
| Manufacturing | 99 | 74 | 91 | 65 | 65 | 60 | 35 | 78 |
| Non-manufacturing | 97 | 73 | 65 | 57 | 53 | 48 | 44 | 94 |

## Life Insurance

Provisions for life insurance are included in 99 percent of the analyzed plans. Maximum coverage of $10,000 or more is called for in 81 percent of the plans specifying amounts of life insurance benefits, up from 74 in the 1986 study, 63 percent in 1983, and 40 percent in 1979. Fourteen percent of these clauses provide coverage ranging from $5,000 to $9,000, and 5 percent offer coverage of less than $5,000.

Under plans specifying benefit amounts, 84 percent of those in manufacturing and 72 percent of those in non-manufacturing provide maximum coverage of $10,000 or more. Employees may purchase additional coverage at their own expense under 36 percent of manufacturing plans and 30 percent of non-manufacturing plans providing for life insurance.

Of programs indicating a formula for determining employees' life insurance benefits, 69 percent provide a flat amount for all employees, 26 percent scale benefits to employees' earnings, and 5 percent scale benefits to length of service.

Service requirements for coverage are included in 65 percent of life insurance provisions. Of the service requirement clauses, 26 percent specify one month, 18 percent specify two months, 35 percent specify three months, and 14 percent specify six months.

More than half (51 percent) of the analyzed life insurance provisions allow employees to change from group to individual coverage upon separation, while 16 percent specify that employees may convert insurance upon retirement, and 6 percent permit conversion upon layoff.

Post-retirement group life insurance coverage, usually paid by the company, is provided in 56 percent of the plans—62 percent in manufacturing and 43 percent in non-manufacturing. Of plans providing post-retirement group coverage, 73 percent state that the amount of coverage declines immediately upon retirement, and 24 percent state that the amount declines gradually.

**Company-paid group coverage during layoffs** is included in 55 percent of manufacturing and 30 percent of non-manufacturing plans providing life insurance benefits. Of plans specifying length of coverage during layoffs, 17 percent extend coverage for one month, 17 percent for three months, 12 percent for six months, 21 percent for one year, and 17 percent for two years; 2 percent state that coverage will last for the duration of the layoff.

**Transition and bridge benefits** are called for in 12 percent of the sample plans—all in manufacturing. A majority (89 percent) of transition provisions specify a set monthly benefit for two years to survivors of covered employees. Bridge benefits usually follow transition benefits and are payable monthly until the survivor either remarries or becomes eligible for social security. Coverage ranges from $100 to $600 per month, with $400 prevailing.

The cost of employees' life insurance coverage is paid by the company under 87 percent of life insurance plans discussing costs, while under 13 percent the cost is shared by the company and the employee. Only 24 percent of surveyed life insurance plans provide coverage for dependents; in all cases the amount of coverage is less than employee coverage. Of plans referring to costs for dependents, coverage is paid by the employer under 41 percent; the employer and employee share costs under 12 percent; and the employee alone pays the costs under 47 percent.

*Industry pattern:* Life insurance coverage is provided in every analyzed plan in manufacturing except for one in transportation equipment and in every plan in non-manufacturing except for one plan each in retail and services.

## Accidental Death and Dismemberment Insurance _____

Coverage for accidental death and dismemberment is provided in 74 percent of the surveyed plans, including 74 percent in manufacturing and 73 percent in non-manufacturing.

Of plans specifying the amount payable in the event of death, 70 percent provide the beneficiary an amount equal to the life insurance benefit, and 17 percent provide an amount equal to half or less of life insurance. Dismemberment payments generally are equal to one-half the life insurance benefit for loss of either a foot, hand, or eye, and the full amount for loss of any two. Under accidental death and dismemberment plans that mention costs, 87 percent state that the cost of the insurance will be paid by the employer.

*Industry pattern:* Accidental death and dismemberment benefits are included in all surveyed plans in construction, leather, maritime, paper, rubber, and stone-clay-glass; and in at least half of all other industries except apparel, communications, petroleum, and utilities.

## Sickness and Accident Insurance _____

Provisions for non-occupational sickness and accident benefits are found in 83 percent of the analyzed plans—91 percent in manufacturing and 65 percent in non-manufacturing.

Of plans that include a formula for sickness and accident benefits, 55 percent call for a flat amount per week. While weekly payments range from $40 to $300, the two most common payments are $150 and $175. Under 27 percent of the benefit formulas, the weekly amount varies according to the pay scale, and under 18 percent, the amount is a fixed percentage of an employee's weekly pay.

Benefits extend for 26 weeks under 38 percent of plans providing S&A insurance and for 52 weeks under 21 percent. Seventy-six percent of S&A plans require a waiting period; sickness benefits most often begin on the eighth day, while accident benefits most often begin on the first day.

Of sickness and accident plans referring to costs, 91 percent specify that coverage will be paid solely by the employer.

*Industry pattern:* Non-occupational sickness and accident benefits are provided in all available plans in apparel, chemicals, furniture, leather, lumber, maritime, mining, primary metals, rubber, and textiles. They appear in at least half of available plans in all other industries except communications, printing, services, and utilities.

S&A benefits extend for 13 weeks in most available plans in leather and textiles; for 26 weeks in most plans in fabricated metals, foods, and paper; and for 52 weeks in most plans in rubber and transportation equipment.

## Occupational Accident Insurance ⎯⎯⎯⎯⎯⎯⎯⎯⎯⎯⎯⎯⎯⎯

Benefits supplementing workers' compensation are included in 27 percent of available plans. Under 62 percent of these provisions, the amount payable is the difference between workers' compensation and the non-occupational sickness and accident rate. All but two plans specifying who will pay for occupational accident insurance state that the employer will pay the full cost.

## Long-Term Disability Insurance ⎯⎯⎯⎯⎯⎯⎯⎯⎯⎯⎯⎯⎯

Benefits that become payable at the expiration of sickness and accident benefits or after a specified period of time are included in 21 percent of the surveyed plans. While the duration of benefits varies considerably, 24 percent of plans dealing with the subject specify payment of benefits until retirement or for the duration of the disability. Four percent pay benefits for life. The cost of insurance most often is paid by the employer.

## Hospitalization Insurance ⎯⎯⎯⎯⎯⎯⎯⎯⎯⎯⎯⎯⎯⎯⎯⎯

Coverage for hospitalization expenses is provided in 63 percent of analyzed plans—65 percent in manufacturing plans and 57 percent in non-manufacturing. Of plans providing hospitalization benefits, 22 percent provide coverage through a service plan such as Blue Cross, while 17 percent state that the plan will be underwritten by a commercial carrier.

More than one-third (35 percent) of the hospitalization provisions permit employees to choose between different types of coverage. In most of these cases, coverage by a health maintenance organization (HMO) or preferred provider organization (PPO) is offered as an alternative to traditional fee-for-service coverage.

Under 78 percent of hospitalization plans detailing coverage, benefits include the total daily room and board charge for a semi-private room. Four percent of the hospitalization coverage provisions base coverage on the hospital's semi-private room rate but set a maximum amount of coverage per day. Eight percent of these clauses set a flat rate per day, with a median of $145.

Duration of hospital benefits is specified in 86 percent of plans outlining hospital insurance coverage. Of these, 44 percent provide coverage for one year, 14 percent each for 120 days and two years, and 12 percent for 70 days.

Coverage for items other than room and board, such as medication, special treatment, and therapy, is mentioned in 81 percent of hospitalization plans detailing benefits. Of plans specifying coverage for extras, 84 percent set no limit, 13 percent limit coverage to a specified amount, and 3 percent pay a specified percentage of charges.

*Hospitalization for dependents* of employees is covered in 98 percent of hospitalization plans. Of these, 99 percent provide coverage equal to that of employees.

The cost of an employee's hospitalization insurance is mentioned in all of the plans. Seventy-eight percent provide that the employer will pay the full cost and 22 percent state that the employer and employee will share the cost. Of plans specifying who will pay for dependent hospitalization coverage, 71 percent provide that the employer will pay the full cost, 2 percent say that the employee will pay the full cost, and 27 percent state that the employer and the employee will share the expense.

*Industry pattern:* Hospitalization insurance is provided in every analyzed plan in apparel, maritime, and rubber, and in at least half of all other industries except chemicals, communications, leather, mining, petroleum, printing, and textiles, where comprehensive plans prevail.

## Surgical Insurance

Surgical insurance is found in 61 percent of the sample plans, including 65 percent in manufacturing and 53 percent in non-manufacturing. Of analyzed plans, 19 percent specify surgical coverage through a service program such as Blue Shield; another 19 percent specify coverage by a commercial carrier. Thirty-five percent of surgical plans grant employees a choice of coverage through a service or commercial plan or through an HMO or PPO.

The amount of surgical benefits is limited to usual and customary rates in 56 percent of plans specifying amounts and is fixed by schedule in 40 percent. Almost one-third (32 percent) of surgical provisions detailing benefits specify a maximum amount of coverage, ranging from $300 to $25,000.

*Surgical insurance for* dependents is discussed in 97 percent of surgical plans and in all cases is equal to employees' coverage.

Of plans specifying who will pay the cost of employees' surgical insurance, 79 percent state that coverage will be paid entirely by the company; the remainder state that the employer and employee will share costs. Under plans mentioning costs for dependent coverage, 70 percent state that the employer will pay, 26 percent provide that the employer and employee will share costs, and 4 percent state that the employee alone will pay for dependent surgical insurance.

*Industry pattern:* Surgical insurance is provided in every available plan in apparel, maritime, and rubber, and is included in at least half of analyzed plans in every industry except chemicals, communications, leather, mining, petroleum, printing and textiles, where comprehensive plans prevail.

## Major Medical Insurance _____

Insurance covering costs in excess of basic hospitalization and surgical insurance is found in 57 percent of the analyzed plans—60 percent in manufacturing and 48 percent in non-manufacturing.

Of major medical programs analyzed, 76 percent specify an initial deductible amount before coverage becomes effective. Forty-eight percent of these provisions specify a $100 deductible per person, 25 percent specify $50, and 21 percent specify more than $100. Of plans mentioning family deductibles, 32 percent specify $300 and 25 percent specify $200.

Ninety-three percent of major medical plans that state the amount of coverage after the deductible contain an 80-20 coinsurance factor, under which the carrier pays 80 percent. Three percent contain a 90-10 factor, 2 percent a 75-25 factor, and another 2 percent specify that the carrier pays all expenses after the deductible.

*A maximum amount of lifetime coverage* is stated in 88 percent of major medical plans detailing coverage, with 24 percent specifying a maximum annual amount and 2 percent specifying a maximum amount per disability. Of plans placing maximums on lifetime coverage, 36 percent specify $300,000 or more, 20 percent provide $250,000, 15 percent call for $100,000, and 8 percent pay $50,000. Eight plans provide unlimited lifetime major medical coverage. Of plans placing annual maximums on coverage, less than $30,000 is stipulated in 21 percent, $30,000 in 25 percent, $35,000-$85,000 in 21 percent, and $100,000 or more in 32 percent. Coverage under plans providing a maximum per disability is $50,000 under one plan and $75,000 under another. Thirty-seven percent of the major medical plans permit restoration to maximum coverage after a claim is made.

Employees' coverage is paid by the employer under 79 percent of plans that state who will pay for major medical insurance, while the employer and employee share costs under 21 percent.

Coverage for dependents is considered in 97 percent of major medical plans. All clauses specifying the amount of coverage available to dependents state that benefits will be equal to employees' coverage. The cost of dependents' insurance is paid solely by the company under 71 percent of major medical plans that mention costs, while 27 percent state that the employee and the employer will share the cost.

*Industry pattern:* Major medical coverage is provided in every analyzed plan in rubber, and in at least two-thirds of plans in apparel, fabricated metals, foods, furniture, lumber, primary metals, retail, and stone-clay-glass. Deductibles of $100 per person are required in at least half the surveyed plans in apparel, construction, and lumber. Three plans in foods require a deductible of $200 per person.

## Doctors' Visits Benefits

Doctors' visits, both in and out of the hospital, are covered in 41 percent of the insurance plans studied. Of the 95 percent of doctors' visits provisions mentioning in-hospital visits, 22 percent specify a maximum amount payable for total visits. A flat rate for each visit, usually $10 to $15, is called for in 24 percent of plans providing in-hospital coverage, and a flat rate per day, ranging from $7 to $40, is called for in 22 percent. Fifteen percent limit coverage to reasonable and customary fees.

Out-of-hospital coverage is included in 46 percent of the doctors' visits provisions; 83 percent of these clauses specify that office visits and house calls will be covered.

Dependents' coverage is equal to employees' coverage under most doctors' visits provisions. In 81 percent of the plans that discuss costs of doctors' visits coverage, the employer pays the full cost of employees' coverage, while in 76 percent the employer pays the cost of dependents' coverage.

*Industry pattern:* Doctors' visits coverage is included in all surveyed plans in apparel and rubber, and in at least one-half of the plans in construction, electrical machinery, fabricated metals, foods, paper, services, and utilities.

## Miscellaneous Medical Expense Benefits

Insurance covering medical expenses not necessarily tied to hospitalization is included in 50 percent of plans in the database. Of plans providing miscellaneous medical expense benefits, almost all (94 percent) cover X-ray and laboratory fees, 41 percent cover anesthetics, and 36 percent cover ambulance costs. Other medical expenses, such as radiation therapy, bandages, prosthetic devices, rental of wheelchairs and other equipment, and oxygen, are provided in 89 percent of these provisions.

Dependent coverage is provided in 98 percent of miscellaneous expense provisions. In all cases dependent coverage is equal to employee coverage. Under most plans specifying who will pay the cost of coverage for employees and dependents, the employer pays.

*Industry pattern:* Miscellaneous medical expenses are covered in all surveyed plans in apparel and in at least two-thirds of the plans in five other industries: construction, lumber, primary metals, rubber, and transportation equipment.

## Maternity Benefits

Coverage for maternity care is provided in 45 percent of the plans included in the study—49 percent in manufacturing and 36 percent in non-manufacturing. Hospital costs are covered in 75 percent of maternity benefits provisions; surgical costs in 76 percent. More than one-third (35 percent) of the maternity provisions specify that sickness and accident benefits will be paid during absences related to maternity care.

All plans specifying maternity coverage for dependents provide medical coverage equal to that of employees. Of clauses specifying who will pay the cost of employee maternity benefits, 80 percent provide that the employer will pay costs, and the remainder provide that the employer and employee will share costs. Under provisions specifying who will pay the cost of dependent maternity benefits, 73 percent call for the employer to pay costs, 24 percent call for the employer and employee to share costs, and 3 percent call for the employee to pay costs.

*Industry pattern:* Maternity benefits are found in all surveyed plans in apparel and in at least one-half of the surveyed plans in construction, foods, lumber, paper, primary metals, rubber, services, stone-clay-glass, transportation equipment, and utilities.

## Comprehensive Insurance

The percentage of comprehensive plans has increased sharply in the last six years, rising to 37 percent of analyzed plans in this study from 21 percent in 1986 and only 9 percent in 1983. Comprehensive insurance is found in 35 percent of manufacturing plans (up from 18 percent in 1986 and 7 percent in 1983) and in 44 percent of non-manufacturing plans (up from 27 percent in 1986 and 15 percent in 1983).

Of comprehensive plans analyzed, 75 percent specify an initial deductible amount per person before coverage becomes effective. Of these, 38 percent specify a $100 deductible, 25 percent $150, and 23 percent more than $150. Of plans mentioning a family deductible, 14 percent specify $200, 44 percent specify $300, and 28 percent specify an amount greater than $300.

Almost three-quarters (74 percent) of comprehensive plans specifying the amount of coverage provided after the deductible is paid call for 80-20 coinsurance, 18 percent call for 90-10 coinsurance, and 7 percent call for 85-15 coinsurance. Thirty-eight percent of the plans permit restoration to maximum coverage after a claim is made.

Sixty percent of comprehensive plans specify annual maximum out-of-pocket expenditures per individual, after which the plan pays all costs. Of these, 29 percent call for maximum payments of $1,000, and 31 percent specify payments greater then $1,000. Maximum out-of-pocket expenditures for families range from $600 to $5,100, with $1,500 most prevalent.

*A maximum amount of lifetime coverage* is stated in 90 percent of comprehensive plans detailing coverage. Only one plan each specifies a maximum amount of coverage per disability or per year. Of plans specifying maximum lifetime coverage, 33 percent specify $1,000,000, 20 percent specify $500,000, and 18 percent specify $250,000. Four plans provide unlimited lifetime comprehensive medical expense coverage.

Benefits for dependents are equal to those of employees in all comprehensive insurance provisions. The cost of employee coverage is paid by the employer in 72 percent of comprehensive plans that mention the matter, and shared by the employer and the employee under 28 percent. Dependent coverage is paid by the employer under 55 percent of these provisions, and shared by the employer and employee under 44 percent.

*Industry pattern:* Comprehensive medical coverage is provided in at least one-half of analyzed plans in 10 industries: chemicals, communications, construction, insurance and finance, leather, mining, paper, petroleum, printing, and textiles.

## Coordination of Benefits

Provisions prohibiting duplication of medical benefits provided by other employers, groups, or any government are found in 70 percent of plans surveyed. Non-duplication of benefits provided by other group insurance plans is called for in 122 plans, non-duplication of government provided benefits in 80 plans, and coordination with benefits provided by another employer in 70.

## Medical Coverage During Layoff

Continued group health-care coverage during layoffs is stipulated in 55 percent of surveyed plans—62 percent in manufacturing and 37 percent in non-manufacturing. Coverage is extended for periods of time ranging from one month to two-and-one-half years, with one year (21 percent), 3 months (18 percent), 6 months (15 percent), and two years (14 percent) mentioned most frequently.

Costs of continued medical coverage during layoff are borne by the employer under 59 percent of clauses providing such coverage, by the employer and employee under 25 percent, and by the employee alone under 17 percent.

## Health Care Cost Containment

Provisions designed to lower the cost of health care are found in 72 percent of surveyed plans, a steep climb from 55 percent in the 1986 study. Cost containment provisions are found in 75 percent of manufacturing plans (up from 57 percent in 1986) and in 66 percent of non-manufacturing plans (up from 50 percent). Most of these measures are intended to reduce costs associated with hospitalization.

Of health care cost containment clauses, 74 percent pay surgical fees for procedures performed on an outpatient basis at a hospital or at a free-standing facility. Second surgical opinion requirements are found in 73 percent of plans containing cost-saving provisions. Most of these specify payment for a second opinion and for a third opinion if the first two differ. Of second surgical provisions, 76 percent specify that without a second opinion for designated procedures, benefits will be paid at a reduced rate, or not at all.

Provisions designed to reduce the length of hospital stays include coverage for home health care (found in 61 percent of plans with cost containment provisions), coverage for care in a skilled nursing facility (59 percent), and a requirement that non-emergency tests be performed on an outpatient basis before admission (57 percent).

Other health care cost containment provisions found in analyzed plans include coverage for hospice care (41 percent), pre-admission or utilization review (38 percent), and restrictions on weekend admissions (17 percent). Fourteen percent of cost containment provisions provide coverage for use of birthing centers, and 10 percent reward employees who detect hospital billing errors.

Over the past three years the number of plans that raised deductibles is a further indication of the drive to cut health care costs. Of major medical plans requiring a deductible, those specifying an amount of more than $100 per person rose from 12 percent in the 1986 study to 21 percent in the 1989 survey.

*The shift to comprehensive medical plans* from traditional hospital-surgical-major medical plans also may be viewed as a move to stem the tide of rising health care costs. Most comprehensive plans require a front-end deductible, payable before any benefits are paid. Under traditional plans, deductibles usually do not apply until after hospital and surgical benefits are exhausted and major medical goes into effect. Further, deductibles under comprehensive plans generally are higher, with 52 percent specifying more than $100 per person, compared with 21 percent of major medical plans.

*Premium cost-sharing* also has increased significantly over the last three years. The percentage of comprehensive plans requiring workers to share premium costs jumped to 28 percent this year from 19 percent in the 1986 survey. Employee contributions are called for in 22 percent of hospital plans discussing financing (up from 13 percent), in 21 percent of surgical plans (up from 12 percent), and in 21 percent of major medical plans (up from 14 percent).

## Dental Care

The percentage of plans in the database providing dental care coverage continued to rise. Eighty-three percent of the plans included in this study contain dental insurance, compared to 79 percent in the 1986 study, 65 percent in 1983, 41 percent in 1979, and 15 percent in 1975. Dental coverage is found in 78 percent of manufacturing plans and 94 percent of non-manufacturing plans.

Deductibles are specified by 36 percent of dental plans. Of plans requiring a deductible, 48 percent specify $25 and 31 percent specify $50.

Under plans detailing coverage of dental costs, the insurance plan pays a percentage up to a maximum in 68 percent, according to a schedule up to a maximum in 14 percent, and according to a schedule with no maximum in 4 percent. All costs up to a maximum are paid under 4 percent of dental plans.

At least half the dental plans cover X-rays, periodic cleanings and examinations, fillings, extractions, reconstruction (dentures and bridges), endodontics (root canals), periodontia (gum care), and flouride treatments. Orthodontic care is covered in 42 percent of the dental plans.

Coverage is extended to dependents in 93 percent of dental plans and is equal to employees' coverage in all cases. Employees' coverage is paid by the company under 81 percent of dental plans that refer to cost and dependents' coverage is paid by the company under 73 percent.

*Industry pattern:* Dental care is provided in all surveyed plans in chemicals, communications, foods, maritime, mining, petroleum, printing, services, and transportation industries, and in at least two-thirds of all other industries except apparel, furniture, leather, lumber, and textiles.

## Prescription Drugs

Insurance covering prescription drug costs is included in 41 percent of the sample plans, a climb from 35 percent in the 1986 study, 29 percent in 1983, and 24 percent in 1979. A deductible (usually $1 to $3 for each prescription) is specified in 72 percent of these provisions, and 7 percent state that a percentage of the costs will be paid. Dependent coverage is provided under 95 percent of the prescription drug provisions. All of these clauses provide equal coverage for dependents. Employee and dependent coverage is paid by the employer under most prescription drug provisions.

*Industry pattern:* Prescription drug benefits are provided in at least half of the plans in apparel, construction, foods, insurance and finance, maritime, retail, rubber, services, and transportation equipment.

## Optical Care

The percentage of surveyed plans providing insurance covering optical care—including eye examinations, lenses, and frames—rose to 47 percent in this study, up from 40 percent in the 1986 survey, 31 percent in 1983, and only 10 percent in 1979. Optical care is included in 41 percent of manufacturing plans and in 63 percent of non-manufacturing plans.

Coverage is extended to dependents in 89 percent of optical care provisions and is equal to employees' coverage in all cases. In most plans discussing costs of optical insurance, the company pays for both employee and dependent coverage.

*Industry pattern:* Optical benefits are provided in at least half of analyzed plans in 12 industries: apparel, communications, construction, fabricated metals, foods, maritime, primary metals, retail, services, transportation, transportation equipment, and utilities.

## Alcohol and Drug Abuse Benefits

Insurance covering treatment of alcohol and drug abuse is included in 49 percent of the sample plans—a climb from 32 percent in the 1986 study. This coverage is found in 49 percent of manufacturing agreements, up from 30 percent in 1986, and in 47 percent of non-manufacturing contracts, up from 38 percent in 1986. Most plans provide coverage for inpatient treatment in a hospital or rehabilitative facility for up to 30 days.

*Industry pattern:* Insurance covering treatment for alcohol or drug abuse is provided in at least two-thirds of contracts in construction, leather, maritime, petroleum, and utilities.

## Medicare-Related Insurance

Insurance coordinating private plans with Medicare benefits is included in 62 percent of the sample plans—67 percent in manufacturing and 50 percent in non-manufacturing. Of these plans 92 percent provide coverage for dependents. Federal law requires employers to offer the same health insurance coverage to workers aged 65 and older as is offered to younger workers, with the option to select either the employer or Medicare as the primary provider. If the employee chooses Medicare, however, the law stipulates that benefits provided under Medicare may not be supplemented by the employer plan.

The company pays the full cost of employees' Medicare-related benefits in 77 percent of plans that mention costs and the full cost of dependent coverage in 72 percent.

Medicare Part B insurance—the optional part of the program that covers physicians' and other medical services—is provided in 32 percent of the sample plans. Of these, 88 percent offer dependent coverage. In most cases the company pays for both employee and dependent coverage.

*Industry pattern:* Medicare-related insurance is found in at least one-half of the surveyed plans in every industry except printing, retail, and transportation.

## Administration of Insurance Benefits

Administration of insurance plans is discussed in 51 percent of the sample. Of these, 61 percent state that the company is the sole administrator, and 27 percent call for administration by joint company-union trustees. Measures for settling disputes are mentioned in 14 percent of the plans discussing administration; of these 27 percent state that disputes will be resolved jointly by the carrier and the employee, although the company may assist. Under plans discussing settlement of administrative disputes, 53 percent specify that disputes will not be subject to the grievance procedure.

# Employee Insurance Benefits

*(Frequency Expressed as Percentage of Plans)*

| | Life Insurance | A D & D | Sickness and Accident | Hospitalization | Surgical | Major Medical | Doctor's Visits | Misc. Medical Expenses | Comprehensive Medical | Dental | Optical |
|---|---|---|---|---|---|---|---|---|---|---|---|
| ALL INDUSTRIES | 99 | 74 | 83 | 63 | 61 | 57 | 41 | 50 | 37 | 83 | 47 |
| MANUFACTURING | 99 | 74 | 91 | 65 | 65 | 60 | 42 | 53 | 35 | 78 | 41 |
| Apparel | 100 | — | 100 | 100 | 100 | 75 | 100 | 100 | — | 25 | 100 |
| Chemicals | 100 | 70 | 100 | 20 | 20 | 20 | — | 10 | 80 | 100 | 20 |
| Electrical Machinery | 100 | 82 | 91 | 64 | 64 | 64 | 55 | 55 | 36 | 73 | 36 |
| Fabricated Metals | 100 | 71 | 93 | 71 | 71 | 71 | 64 | 57 | 29 | 86 | 50 |
| Foods | 100 | 50 | 92 | 67 | 58 | 67 | 50 | 50 | 33 | 100 | 67 |
| Furniture | 100 | 67 | 100 | 67 | 67 | 67 | 33 | 33 | 33 | 33 | 33 |
| Leather | 100 | 100 | 100 | 33 | 33 | 33 | — | — | 67 | — | — |
| Lumber | 100 | 50 | 100 | 75 | 75 | 75 | 25 | 75 | 25 | 25 | 25 |
| Machinery | 100 | 75 | 95 | 55 | 55 | 55 | 35 | 50 | 45 | 85 | 35 |
| Paper | 100 | 100 | 88 | 50 | 50 | 38 | 50 | 50 | 50 | 88 | 13 |
| Petroleum | 100 | 33 | 67 | 33 | 33 | 33 | — | 33 | 67 | 100 | — |
| Primary Metals | 100 | 75 | 100 | 81 | 81 | 81 | 44 | 75 | 19 | 88 | 50 |
| Printing | 100 | 67 | 33 | 33 | 33 | 33 | — | — | 67 | 100 | 33 |
| Rubber | 100 | 100 | 100 | 100 | 100 | 100 | 100 | 80 | — | 80 | 40 |
| Stone, Clay & Glass | 100 | 100 | 89 | 78 | 78 | 78 | 44 | 56 | 22 | 67 | 33 |
| Textiles | 100 | 83 | 100 | 33 | 33 | 33 | 17 | 17 | 67 | 50 | — |
| Transportation Equipment | 95 | 81 | 76 | 86 | 86 | 57 | 43 | 71 | 14 | 81 | 62 |
| NON-MANUFACTURING | 97 | 73 | 65 | 57 | 53 | 48 | 37 | 40 | 44 | 94 | 63 |
| Communications | 100 | 25 | 25 | — | — | — | — | — | 100 | 100 | 50 |
| Construction | 100 | 100 | 50 | 50 | 50 | 50 | 50 | 75 | 50 | 75 | 75 |
| Insurance & Finance | 100 | 75 | 75 | 50 | 50 | 50 | 25 | 25 | 50 | 75 | 25 |
| Maritime | 100 | 100 | 100 | 100 | 100 | 33 | 33 | — | — | 100 | 67 |
| Mining | 100 | 83 | 100 | 17 | 17 | 17 | 17 | 17 | 83 | 100 | — |
| Retail | 92 | 92 | 92 | 69 | 54 | 69 | 46 | 62 | 31 | 92 | 92 |
| Services | 90 | 80 | 40 | 70 | 70 | 50 | 60 | 60 | 30 | 100 | 70 |
| Transportation | 100 | 54 | 62 | 62 | 62 | 54 | 23 | 31 | 39 | 100 | 69 |
| Utilities | 100 | 40 | 20 | 60 | 60 | 60 | 60 | 40 | 40 | 80 | 60 |

## Employee Insurance Benefits

*(Frequency Expressed as Percentage of Plans in Each Region)*

| | Life Insurance | A D & D | Sickness and Accident | Hospitalization | Surgical | Major Medical | Doctor's Visits | Misc. Medical Expenses | Comprehensive Medical | Dental | Optical |
|---|---|---|---|---|---|---|---|---|---|---|---|
| ALL REGIONS | 99 | 74 | 83 | 63 | 61 | 57 | 41 | 50 | 37 | 83 | 47 |
| Middle Atlantic | 97 | 63 | 82 | 76 | 74 | 71 | 47 | 47 | 24 | 92 | 53 |
| Midwest | 100 | 83 | 89 | 44 | 44 | 44 | 39 | 44 | 56 | 89 | 56 |
| New England | 100 | 100 | 100 | 85 | 85 | 85 | 62 | 46 | 15 | 77 | 39 |
| North Central | 98 | 74 | 90 | 54 | 54 | 49 | 28 | 47 | 46 | 70 | 33 |
| Rocky Mountain | 100 | 100 | 100 | 100 | 100 | 100 | 100 | — | — | 100 | — |
| Southeast | 96 | 76 | 92 | 52 | 52 | 52 | 28 | 48 | 48 | 68 | 16 |
| Southwest | 100 | 100 | 80 | 40 | 40 | 40 | 40 | 40 | 60 | 80 | 60 |
| West Coast | 100 | 80 | 40 | 60 | 50 | 40 | 45 | 45 | 40 | 95 | 65 |
| Multiregion | 100 | 62 | 84 | 73 | 73 | 62 | 51 | 65 | 27 | 95 | 73 |

# 4

## Pensions

Almost all contracts included in the Basic Patterns sample make some reference to pension plans. Some agreements simply contain a statement referring to an existing program maintained by the employer or to the amount the employer is required to contribute to a trusteed fund, while others contain fully detailed plans.

Where full detail is stated, a typical plan provides for normal, early, and disability retirement, specifying eligibility requirements and benefits available in each case. Vesting provisions, administrative procedures, and financing arrangements also commonly are covered.

The following analysis is based on 165 plans for which sufficient detail was available. Fifty of these plans are multi-employer plans financed by fixed employer contributions.

### Normal Retirement

A normal retirement age is specified in all but five of the 165 available plans. Age 65 is stipulated in 91 percent of these plans; normal retirement ages range from 60 to 70 in the remainder. In 49 of the 51 plans stating a compulsory retirement age, age 70 is stipulated.

A Jan. 1, 1987, amendment to the Age Discrimination in Employment Act outlawed mandatory retirement at age 70, or at any age. If retirement at age 70 was specified in employee benefit plans under collective bargaining contracts in effect June 30, 1986, and terminating after Jan. 1, 1987, the legislation deferred the prohibition of mandatory retirement until expiration of the agreements, or Jan. 1, 1990, whichever occurred first.

Minimum service requirements are called for in 79 of the available plans. Of these provisions, 66 percent require 10 years of service, and 17 percent require 5 years.

Limitations are placed on the amount of service that may be credited for pension purposes in 22 of the plans studied. Of the plans with limitations on service credits, seven stipulate 25 years; six stipulate 35 years; five stipulate 30 years; three call for 40 years; and one states 37 years.

Federal regulations issued pursuant to the above 1987 amendment, prohibit limitations on the number of credited years of service. Collectively bargained plans were given until 1990 to comply.

### Service Requirements in Years

*(Frequency Expressed as Percentage of 79 Plans Stating Minimums)*

| Years' Service | 1-5 | 6-10 | 11-15 | 16-20 | 25 or more |
|---|---|---|---|---|---|
| Percentage | 19 | 67 | 6 | 1 | 6 |

Benefit formulas are included in all but three plans surveyed. Fifty-three percent of benefit formulas guarantee a flat dollar amount a month for each year of service. Under 15 percent of these provisions (mainly in the automobile industry) the monthly amount varies according to base rates or classifications. The monthly flat benefits per year of service range from $2.55 to $54.54 (with a median of about $18.63). The most common monthly benefits in plans with this formula are $20 per year of service (11 percent), $18 and $17 (each 6 percent), and $16 (5 percent).

In the 1986 survey, the most common benefit also was $20 (11 percent), followed by $16 (10 percent), $17 (7 percent), and $15 (6 percent). The median was about $16.85.

### Number of Plans Providing Flat Monthly Benefit Per Year of Service

|                | $5 or less | $5.20-$10 | $10.20-$15 | $15.20-$20 | $20.20 or more |
|----------------|------------|-----------|------------|------------|----------------|
| Mfg.           | 2          | 5         | 17         | 25         | 21             |
| Non-Mfg.       | 2          | —         | —          | 5          | 9              |
| All Industries | 4          | 5         | 17         | 30         | 30             |

Eighteen of the plans studied compute benefits as a percentage of employees' earnings multiplied by their years of service. Under 10 of these, employees' earnings during their entire period of credited service are taken into consideration; in the remaining eight, the percentage is applied to the employee's average earnings during the most recent (or highest paid) period of service—the ten years preceding retirement, for example.

Under three of the plans, the benefit is the greater of the amounts arrived at under alternative formulas—either a flat dollar amount multiplied by years of service or a percentage of earnings.

In the 50 multi-employer plans included in the study, benefit levels usually are determined by the trustees according to the amount of money in the trust fund. Employees' benefits, commonly stated in a flat amount per month, vary according to their years of service in the industry and the amount of contributions paid into their account.

Five percent of the sample plans integrate Social Security benefits in computing pensions. Cost-of-living adjustments for retirees are found in only six plans studied (down from 14 in the 1986 study). Under 21 plans, benefits were increased for retirees.

Contingent annuitant options, whereby an employee may elect to receive a reduced pension which is continued and payable to a spouse or dependent after the employee's death, are specified in all but three plans surveyed.

Survivor benefits, payable if an employee dies before reaching normal retirement age, are provided in 92 percent of the plans studied (unchanged from the 1986 analysis).

## Disability Retirement

Pension benefits for employees forced to retire due to total and permanent disability are provided in 90 percent of the plans studied. While 11 percent of disability pension clauses specify a minimum age requirement (40 and 50 being the most common), the majority merely state that an employee must be under normal or early retirement age. Eighty-nine percent of disability provisions contain a service requirement—23 percent of these call for 15 years and 62 percent for 10 years.

An eligibility waiting period for disability benefits is imposed in 47 percent of the disability provisions. Under these clauses, the most common waiting period (56 percent) is six months.

Forty-eight percent of the plans specifying amounts of disability pensions employ the same formula used for computing normal benefits. Larger than normal benefits—until the disabled pensioner becomes eligible for normal retirement or social security benefits—are provided in 20 percent of the plans with disability pension formulas. Under 12 percent of the formulas, disability benefits are less than normal benefits.

Grounds for loss of disability benefits are stated in 28 percent of the plans. Of penalty provisions, 38 percent disqualify recipients engaging in any gainful occupation, and 81 percent disqualify those refusing to submit to a medical examination.

Of the 149 plans calling for disability pensions, 49 specify that payments will continue until the retiree is eligible for normal benefits, and 15 state that payments will continue until the retiree is eligible for Social Security benefits.

Disability benefit deductions are mentioned in 40 of the surveyed plans. The most common deductions are other pensions (11 plans) and workmen's compensation (26 plans).

*Industry pattern:* All manufacturing plans included in the study contain disability retirement provisions except transportation equipment (94 percent), fabricated metals (92 percent), foods (91 percent), primary metals (90 percent), stone-clay-glass (86 percent), paper, rubber, and textiles (each 75 percent), and chemicals (71 percent). All non-manufacturing plans contain these provisions except mining (80 percent), services (78 percent), and utilities (25 percent).

## Early Retirement

Voluntary early retirement is allowed in 96 percent of the plans. While plans frequently contain several programs for early retirement, this study deals only with typical—age and service—programs.

In 95 percent of plans with early retirement provisions included in this study, an age requirement is specified. Of these, 57 percent stipulate age 55, 23 percent age 60, 11 percent age 62, and 5 percent age 50. A service requirement is stated in 89 percent of early retirement provisions. Under service requirement provisions, the most common requirement is 10 years (65 percent), followed by 15 years (21 percent), and five, 20, and 30 years (each 4 percent).

Benefits usually are proportionately reduced by the number of years an employee is under the normal retirement age. An immediate pension based on credited service at the time of retirement and reduced on the basis of age is called for in 91 percent of early retirement provisions. Twenty-nine percent of early retirement provisions give employees the option of immediate reduced benefits or unreduced benefits at age 65 based on credited service. Twenty-six percent of the provisions studied call for some type of "30 and out" formula permitting retirement after 30 years of service regardless of age.

*Industry Pattern:* All plans included in the analysis contain voluntary early retirement provisions except stone-clay-glass (86 percent), fabricated metals (83 percent), maritime (80 percent), services (78 percent), and paper (75 percent).

***Special early retirement*** benefits for employees retired by mutual consent or displaced by a plant shutdown or layoff are found in 28 percent of plans contained in this study. Of these provisions, 59 percent permit special early retirement because of plant shutdown, 54 percent if mutually agreed, and 33 percent at employer option.

Age requirements are specified in 61 percent of the special early retirement provisions with age 55 predominating—57 percent, followed by age 50 at 21 percent. Service requirements appear in 83 percent of the provisions with 10 years being the most common (45 percent), followed 15 years (18 percent). Age plus service requirements—whereby an employee's age and years of service combined must total a specified number—are included in 28 percent of special early retirement provisions.

Under 48 percent of plans permitting special early retirement, an employee is entitled to a larger-than-normal benefit which is reduced upon reaching eligibility for normal retirement or Social Security. Normal retirement benefits are provided under 20 of these provisions (down from 26 percent in 1986).

*Industry pattern:* Special early retirement provisions are included mainly in manufacturing plans contained in the database—furniture 75 percent, transportation equipment 72 percent, and rubber and machinery each 50 pecent.

# Vesting

Vesting provisions, under which an employee whose service is terminated remains entitled to earned benefits, are spelled out in 159 of the 165 plans included in this study. Full vesting programs, under which total earned benefits are vested after a maximum 10 years' service, are specified in 144 sample plans. Thirteen plans contain graduated vesting programs, under which accrued benefits initially are partly vested and gradually become fully vested.

Amendments to the Employee Retirement Income Security Act require vesting under one of three formulas beginning Jan. 1, 1989, and by no later than Jan. 1, 1991, for collectively bargained plans. In single-employer plans, 100 percent vesting is required after five years of service or after seven years of service where vesting is graduated. In multi-employer plans, full vesting is required after 10 years for participants covered by collective bargaining agreements.

*Portability provisions,* which allow employees to change jobs and remain covered by a pension plan and build up credits as long as they work for a contributing employer, appear only in multi-employer plans.

# Determination of Credited Service

Under most plans, credited service for pension purposes is divided into two distinct parts—credit for service prior to the effective date of a new or revised plan and credit for service subsequent to the effective date. As a rule, past service is at least equal to seniority as determined under the collective bargaining agreement. In those single-employer plans that define future service, 49 base this computation on continuous service—"continuous service" being roughly equal to seniority. Under another 58 plans, future service is based on the number of hours worked or paid for each year. Of these, the most common hours-worked requirements are 1,000 (36 percent), followed by 1,700 (17 percent), 1,800 (12 percent), and 2,000 (9 percent). Of the plans with hours requirements, 60 percent give partial credit if the requirement for full credit is not met.

In multi-employer plans, determination of credited service varies, but generally it is based on a combination of number of years' service in the industry and number of hours or days worked for a contributing employer.

# Financing and Funding of Pensions

Of the plans for which details are available, 94 percent are non-contributory—that is, entirely financed by the employer. In the remainder costs are shared in varying degrees by employers and employees.

Single-employer contributory plans invariably state exactly how much the employee must contribute, while multi-employer non-contributory plans state how much the employer must contribute. Both contributory and non-contributory single-employer plans, however, are written on the basis of benefits rather than costs. In these, where reference is made to the employer's contribution, the majority stipulate that contributions must be sufficient—as determined by a qualified actuary—to finance the specified benefits.

Funding of pension plan obligations already incurred by setting aside set sums of money in equal annual installments over a prescribed period of time and funding of normal costs for the plan year on a current basis are required by law.

## Administration and Termination of Plans

Of the single-employer plans containing administrative procedures, a majority specifies management control, while the remainder specifies joint board control, usually over such matters as procedures and disputes concerning eligibility or applications for pension benefits. All multi-employer plans are jointly administered.

Plan termination is referred to in 81 percent of the plans included in this study. Usually such provisions specify how the existing fund will be distributed among plan participants.

# 5

# Grievances and Arbitration

Grievance and arbitration provisions are found in all 400 contracts contained in CBNC's Basic Patterns database.

Grievance procedures generally follow a relatively standard pattern. Complaints usually are processed through a succession of steps, progressing from lower to higher management and union representatives. In most cases, unresolved disputes proceed through arbitration for resolution by an impartial third party.

Variations occur in the scope of grievance and arbitration systems, the method of presenting and responding to complaints, the number of steps, and the overall complexity of dispute procedures.

## Grievance Procedures

Grievance procedures are contained in all but one of the contracts analyzed; under that contract, disputes are referred directly to arbitration.

**The scope of the grievance procedure** is specified in 91 percent of the sample agreements. Of these, 79 percent permit grievances over any interpretation or application of the contract. In 13 percent of the contracts specifying scope, the grievance procedure encompasses any matter regarding wages, hours, or working conditions. Specific disputes are covered under the grievance procedure in 46 percent of these provisions, while specific complaints are excluded in 29 percent.

## Steps In Grievance Procedures

*(Frequency Expressed as Percentage of Contracts Specifying Steps)*

|  | Number of Steps | | | | |
|---|---|---|---|---|---|
|  | 1 | 2 | 3 | 4 | 5 |
| All Industries | 7 | 21 | 48 | 21 | 3 |
| Manufacturing | 2 | 13 | 54 | 27 | 4 |
| Non-manufacturing | 14 | 34 | 40 | 11 | 2 |

**Number of steps** is specified in 99 percent of contracts analyzed. Three-step procedures are most common (48 percent), followed by four-step and two-step procedures (each 21 percent), and one-step (7 percent). Five-step systems are outlined in 12 agreements, and six-step systems are called for in two agreements.

## First-Step Procedures

Formal first-step procedures are detailed in 96 percent of the sample contracts. Of these, 48 percent give an employee the option of presenting a grievance alone or in the presence of a union representative. Twenty-one percent of first-step procedures state that a grievant will be accompanied by a union representative when presenting a formal grievance, and 20 percent state that grievances are to be presented by a union representative.

Grievances most often are initiated with an employee's immediate supervisor (43 percent of contracts specifying first-step procedures) or with the shop foreman (29 percent).

*The manner of first-step presentation* is specified in 59 percent of agreements analyzed. Under 51 percent of these provisions, a grievance must be presented in writing, while in the remainder, presentation may be made orally. Management's manner of response is detailed in 39 percent of the sample contracts. In 60 percent of these clauses, a written response is required, and in the rest an oral response is sufficient.

*Time limits for filing grievances* in the first step vary from one day to six months and appear in 66 percent of contracts studied. Under these provisions, the most common time limits for presenting a grievance to management are five days (23 percent), 30 days (20 percent), 10 days (16 percent), and 15 days (9 percent).

*Time limits for management's response* at the first step are specified in 53 percent of agreements and vary from one day to 60 days. Management is required to respond after two days in 26 percent of time-limit provisions; after three days in 21 percent; after five days in 19 percent; and after one day in 18 percent. Five percent of time-limit provisions require a response after 10 days, and another 5 percent require a response after seven days.

## Union and Management Grievances

Thirty-six percent of sample contracts state that the union may file grievances on its own behalf. These grievances usually deal with management practices or changes affecting a large number of employees or with rights specifically granted to the union under the contract. Management's right to file a grievance is mentioned in 30 percent of the sample.

*Industry pattern:* Unions are granted access to the grievance machinery in 39 percent of non-manufacturing contracts and 34 percent of manufacturing agreements. Industries in which at least one-half of contracts permit unions to file grievances on their own behalf include insurance and finance (71 percent) and mining and rubber (each 50 percent). At least one-third of the agreements in 14 other industries similarly permit unions to file grievances.

Management is permitted to file grievances in 36 percent of non-manufacturing and 26 percent of manufacturing contracts. Management retains the right to file grievances in 56 percent of service-industry contracts, and in one-half of agreements in the rubber and furniture industries. In five other industries, management's right to initiate grievances is specified in at least one-third of contracts.

## Appellate Levels in Grievance Procedures

Special requirements for processing complaints beyond the first step in the grievance procedure are included in 85 percent of sample contracts. Of these provisions, 82 percent specify that the grievance must be presented in writing at subsequent steps, 79 percent set time limits for union appeals to higher steps, 82 percent set time limits for management's response, and 69 percent require that management submit a response in writing.

Thirty-nine percent of sample contracts specify that if the union or employer fails to respond to a grievance within a specified time limit, the grievance automatically is settled in favor of the other party.

*Bypassing of one or more steps* or special handling for certain grievances is provided for in 72 percent of the 400 agreements. Under these provisions, grievances most frequently are initiated at a higher step or receive special handling when they concern discharges (78 percent), suspensions (47 percent), general policy or group grievances (30 percent), grievances filed by management (17 percent), or safety and health issues (13 percent). Fifty-three percent of these clauses provide for expedited or special handling for a variety of other disputes, such as grievances over incentive rates and time studies.

*Industry pattern:* Expedited or special handling of certain grievances is specified in 76 percent of manufacturing and 65 percent of non-manufacturing agreements. This provision is found in at least three-fourths of apparel, electrical machinery, petroleum, transportation, machinery, paper, primary metals, rubber, transportation equipment, mining, maritime, insurance and finance, and fabricated metals agreements.

*Representatives at mid-level steps* are designated in 69 percent of agreements in the database. Most frequently, union representatives handling grievances at mid-level steps are members of an in-company grievance committee (43 percent of these provisions) or shop stewards (20 percent). An international union representative is designated in 4 percent of these clauses, and the local union president is named in another 4 percent. Management often is represented at mid-level grievance meetings by industrial relations personnel (27 percent of clauses dealing with the subject) or by the plant manager or the manager's representative (18 percent). In 11 percent of provisions specifying representatives, grievances are handled by a department head, while in another 7 percent a foreman handles mid-level grievances.

*Joint company/union grievance meetings* are provided for in 28 percent of contracts studied. These meetings generally are held to discuss mid-level grievances and are part of the formal grievance procedure. Meetings are scheduled weekly under 26 percent of the contracts calling for joint meetings, monthly under 19 percent, and every two weeks under 11 percent. Fourteen percent of these clauses provide for "regularly scheduled" meetings.

*Final-step representatives* are specified in 80 percent of agreements. Under these provisions, union representatives at the final step are listed with the following frequency: international representatives (37 percent); in-company grievance committees (23 percent); local presidents (4 percent); and international union presidents (3 percent). Management representatives at the final step most frequently named in provisions dealing with the subject are industrial relations directors (38 percent); plant managers (11 percent); and top executive officers of the company (9 percent).

## Union Grievance Representatives

Restrictions are placed on grievance representatives in 40 percent of contracts analyzed, more frequently in manufacturing (54 percent) than in nonmanufacturing agreements (18 percent). Of these, 69 percent limit the number of grievance representatives and 12 percent limit the activity of grievance representatives on company time. Sixteen percent of these clauses place limitations on both the number and activity of representatives.

*Special job security provisions* (not superseniority) are included in 36 percent of agreements studied. Forty-five percent of these contracts prohibit management from discriminating against grievance representatives or interfering with their activities, and 46 percent grant shift- overtime- or holiday work-preference for union representatives.

*Industry pattern:* Special job security provisions for grievance representatives are included in 36 percent of manufacturing and 35 percent of non-manufacturing contracts. At least one-half of contracts in the textiles, furniture, machinery, transportation equipment, and construction industries provide some form of job security to grievance representatives. Further, at least one-third of retail, primary metals, and electrical machinery agreements contain such clauses.

*Pay provisions for union representatives* who present, investigate, or handle grievances are specified in 55 percent of contracts in the database. The number of hours for which management pays grievance representatives is limited in 17 percent of these clauses. Twenty-three percent of contracts dealing with the subject contain a general statement that paid time will not be "unreasonable or excessive."

*Industry pattern:* Pay provisions for union grievance investigators are included in 67 percent of manufacturing agreements and in 34 percent of non-manufacturing contracts. Compensation is granted to grievance representatives in all contracts in the rubber and furniture industries, and in at least three-fourths of contracts in machinery, fabricated metals, electrical machinery, leather, transportation equipment, and chemicals. More than one-half of contracts in mining, textiles, primary metals, paper, petroleum, stone-clay-glass, communications, and utilities specify pay for grievance procedure activity.

## Conciliation and Mediation

Only 14 of the 400 sample contracts call for conciliation and/or mediation. Under 12 of these agreements, conciliation/mediation is an intermediate step between grievance and arbitration; under the remaining two, it is the final step in the grievance procedure.

## Arbitration

Arbitration is called for in 98 percent of the sample contracts—99 percent in manufacturing and 96 percent in non-manufacturing.

*Industry pattern:* Arbitration provisions appear in all contracts in all industries with the exception of construction (93 percent), retail (96 percent), transportation (88 percent), and lumber (86 percent).

**The scope of arbitration** is specified in 95 percent of the sample. Of these provisions, 92 percent provide for arbitration of any dispute not resolved through the grievance procedure. Specific issues are excluded from arbitration procedures in 36 percent of these contracts; specific issues are included in 28 percent. In 5 percent of provisions specifying scope of arbitration, certain matters bypass the grievance procedure and go directly to arbitration.

**Initiation procedures** are described in 97 percent of the contracts studied. Of these provisions, 90 percent state that arbitration may be invoked at the request of either party; 9 percent stipulate that arbitration automatically follows the grievance procedure. Mutual agreement of the parties is required to proceed to arbitration under less than 1 percent of initiation clauses.

**Time limits on appealing a grievance** to arbitration are included in 73 percent of the 400 contracts and range from one day to six months. Under these provisions, the most frequent time limits specified are 30 days (27 percent), 10 days (19 percent), 15 days (14 percent), five days (8 percent), 20 days (5 percent), and seven days (4 percent).

"Justice and dignity" procedures designed to expedite arbitration proceedings in discharge and discipline cases are called for in 10 of the 400 sample agreements. These provisions allow employees to remain on the job until a determination of the case is made by an arbitrator. Of the contracts containing such clauses, six are in the primary metals industry, three are contained in fabricated metals, and one is in mining.

## Selection of Arbitrator

*(Frequency Expressed as Percentage of Contracts Specifying Selection)*

| Selection Process | All Industries | Manufacturing | Non-manufacturing |
|---|---|---|---|
| Single Arbitrator Appointed by Contract | 5 | 7 | 2 |
| Permanent Board Appointed by Contract | 1 | 1 | 1 |
| List of Arbitrators, Serving on Rotating Basis | 5 | 5 | 6 |
| Ad Hoc, Selected by Parties | 45 | 44 | 46 |
| Ad Hoc, via Facilities of Impartial Party | 29 | 32 | 25 |

*Selection of an arbitrator* is detailed in 96 percent of the agreements analyzed. In 45 percent of the contracts specifying a method of selection, the arbitrator is chosen on an ad hoc basis by the parties, and in 29 percent, the arbitrator is selected on an ad hoc basis through the facilities of an impartial agency (generally from a list of arbitrators supplied by the agency). Under 6 percent of selection clauses, a permanent arbitration board is appointed, or a list of arbitrators, who serve on a rotating basis, is included in the agreement. A single arbitrator is appointed to serve for the duration of the contract in 5 percent of the provisions.

Under 50 percent of contracts specifying the selection process, an impartial agency is used to select the arbitrator if the parties reach an impasse in the selection process or if the chosen arbitrator is unavailable. The Federal Mediation and Conciliation Service is the impartial agency used in 60 percent of these clauses, followed by the American Arbitration Association (29 percent). Twelve percent of these provisions specify other impartial agencies, including state or federal courts, or state mediation agencies.

*The number of arbitrators* is specified in 94 percent of the sample agreements. In 79 percent of these contracts the services of a single arbitrator are employed, while in 15 percent, three arbitrators (usually an impartial chairman selected by one arbiter chosen by management and one chosen by the union) are specified. Six percent of agreements indicating the number of arbiters call for a five-member arbitration board.

*Industry pattern:* Of contracts discussing the number of arbitrators, a majority of both manufacturing (88 percent) and non-manufacturing (65 percent) contracts specify a single arbiter. All agreements in the paper, fabricated metals, mining, apparel, stone-clay-glass, and leather industries call for a single arbitrator. In addition, all but one of the contracts in the maritime, rubber, furniture, lumber, and textiles industries call for one arbiter. A majority of petroleum, transportation, and utilities industry contracts specify three-member arbitration boards.

*Determination of arbitrability* of a dispute is addressed in only 41 of the sample agreements. In all but six of these contracts, the decision as to whether a dispute is properly before an arbitrator is left to the arbiter selected to hear the case.

*Restrictions are placed on arbitrators* in 82 percent of agreements studied. Of these, 92 percent apply a general restriction prohibiting the arbitrator from adding to, subtracting from, or in any way altering contract language. Twenty-five percent of restrictive clauses specify that arbitrators must submit their decisions in writing, and 38 percent require that decisions be rendered within a specified time period, usually 30 days.

*Retroactivity of an arbitrator's award* is mentioned in 32 percent of agreements in the database. Of these, 45 percent limit retroactivity to a specified point prior to the filing of the grievance, 21 percent limit retroactivity to the point of filing the grievance, and 3 percent limit retroactivity to the point of occurrence of the action giving rise to the grievance.

*Arbitration expense provisions* are found in 91 percent of the sample. Under 92 percent of these provisions, the fee is shared equally by the parties. Where a multiple-member arbitration board is used, the parties generally assume the costs of their own representatives on the board, and share the fee of the impartial chairman. In 4 percent of expense clauses, the fee is paid by the losing party.

Collateral expenses (for example, copies of transcripts of arbitration hearings) are discussed in 20 percent of contracts containing arbitration expense provisions. Under 55 percent of these clauses, costs are shared equally, and under 31 percent, the costs are paid by the party requesting transcripts or other services.

Eighteen percent of expense provisions refer to pay for time lost by witnesses at an arbitration hearing; most provide for reimbursement by the calling party.

# Grievance and Arbitration Provisions

*(Frequency Expressed as Percentage of Contracts in Each Region)*

| | All Regions | Middle Atlantic | Midwest | New England | North Central | Rocky Mountain | Southeast | Southwest | West Coast | Multiregion |
|---|---|---|---|---|---|---|---|---|---|---|
| Grievance Procedure | 99 | 100 | 100 | 100 | 99 | 100 | 100 | 100 | 100 | 100 |
| Scope of Grievance Procedure | 91 | 94 | 92 | 84 | 89 | 70 | 96 | 100 | 94 | 90 |
| Union May File | 36 | 36 | 29 | 40 | 33 | 40 | 28 | 39 | 44 | 43 |
| Company May File | 30 | 36 | 25 | 36 | 25 | 40 | 20 | 31 | 35 | 32 |
| Restrictions on Grievance Reps | 40 | 34 | 38 | 32 | 48 | 20 | 50 | 54 | 37 | 37 |
| Job Security For Grievance Reps | 36 | 39 | 29 | 28 | 46 | 40 | 26 | 39 | 37 | 28 |
| Pay For Investigation | 55 | 53 | 42 | 52 | 71 | 40 | 62 | 54 | 24 | 58 |
| Conciliation | 4 | 5 | 8 | — | 5 | — | 4 | — | 2 | 2 |
| Arbitration | 98 | 98 | 96 | 100 | 99 | 100 | 100 | 100 | 96 | 98 |
| Scope of Arbitration | 95 | 95 | 96 | 100 | 96 | 80 | 94 | 100 | 89 | 95 |
| Restrictions on Arbitrators | 82 | 82 | 71 | 80 | 83 | 100 | 90 | 77 | 80 | 80 |
| Arbitration Expenses | 91 | 87 | 92 | 96 | 96 | 90 | 94 | 100 | 91 | 85 |

# 6

# Income Maintenance

Income maintenance provisions are found in 52 percent of the Basic Patterns database sample. The three major types of income protection are work or pay guarantees, severance pay, and supplemental unemployment benefit plans. Geographic analysis shows that income maintenance guarantees are most common in the mid-Atlantic and multiregion contracts.

### Trend in Income Maintenance Provisions
*(Frequency Expressed as Percentage of Contracts)*

|  | 1966 | 1971 | 1975 | 1979 | 1983 | 1986 | 1989 |
|---|---|---|---|---|---|---|---|
| Income maintenance provisions | 38 | 40 | 48 | 49 | 51 | 52 | 52 |
| Work or pay guarantees | 6 | 5 | 6 | 9 | 11 | 13 | 13 |
| Severance pay provisions | 29 | 34 | 39 | 37 | 39 | 41 | 40 |
| SUB plans * | 14 | 15 | 17 | 16 | 16 | 16 | 14 |

\* SUB percentages include unavailable plans.

## Guarantees of Work or Pay

Work or pay guarantees are called for in 51 contracts. Of the 37 contracts calling for weekly guarantees, 24 guarantee 40 hours per week, nine call for 35 to 38 hours, one calls for 32 hours, and one provides for 15 hours. Two agreements specify a minimum amount of weekly pay, without reference to hours. In eight contracts the weekly guarantee is reduced during holiday weeks.

Monthly guarantees appear in two agreements. One provides a certain number of hours of work or pay per month, and one guarantees a percentage of average monthly pay. Three contracts in the study provide annual guarantees of one year each. Also contained in the sample are two contracts guaranteeing employment for the life of the agreement, and four contracts specifying a lifetime guarantee. A variety of long-term guarantees, guaranteed annual income streams for high-seniority workers and guarantees of work or pay for jobs lost to subcontracting, are found in the three major auto industry contracts.

More than three-fifths (62 precent) of work or pay guarantees cover all regular employees; one-quarter require a minimum amount of service. Guarantees may be voided under 26 contracts, generally in the event of a strike, lack of work for reasons beyond an employer's control, acts of God, or time absent without cause.

*Industry pattern:* Guarantees appear in 6 percent of contracts in manufacturing and 23 percent of agreements in non-manufacturing. Twelve guarantee provisions are found in retail, 11 in transportation, seven in foods, five in services, four each in maritime and transportation equipment, three in printing, two in utilities, and one each in construction, insurance and finance, and textiles.

Weekly guarantees are concentrated in foods, retail, services, and transportation. Two agreements in transportation contain monthly guarantees. Annual guarantees are found in two maritime agreements and one utilities agreement. Lifetime guarantees appear in three printing contracts and one transportation agreement. Two contracts guaranteeing jobs for the life of the contract are found in retail.

## Severance Pay

Severance or separation pay, provided for under 40 percent of the sample, may be awarded in a lump sum either upon termination, or after a specified period of time, or in installments. These provisions are found in 45 percent of manufacturing contracts and 33 percent of non-manufacturing agreements. Although many severance pay clauses are part of SUB plans, they are treated separately in this section.

Employees terminated as a result of a permanent shutdown are eligible for severance pay under 52 percent of severance plans studied. Severance is payable to employees on layoff for a minimum length of time in 17 percent of the provisions; to employees on layoff with no prospect of recall in 17 percent; and to employees on any layoff or on layoff for unspecified reasons in 24 percent. Three percent of these plans call for severance pay at retirement, and 12 percent provide severance for employees who are ineligible for pensions. Severance is payable for other reasons under 26 percent of the provisions.

The most common method for determining the amount of severance benefit—found in 74 percent of severance provisions—is a schedule based on service and earnings. Just over two-thirds (67 percent) of provisions basing severance on service and earnings call for graduated schedules that increase the number of weeks' pay as length of service increases. The remainder provide a specific number of weeks' pay per year of service. Of those providing a specific number of weeks' pay for each year of service, 78 percent call for one week's pay, 7 percent provide one-half weeks' pay, and another 5 percent provide two weeks' pay (the maximum amount found in this study).

Eight percent of severance provisions pay a flat weekly sum per year of service. While weekly pay ranges from $30 to $300 a week per year of service, the most common amount is $100. Under 5 percent of severance plans studied, pay is based solely on earnings. The majority determine amounts of pay by other means or do not specify a method of determining the amounts.

*Limitations on the duration of severance pay* are imposed in 49 percent of severance provisions and range from two to 104 weeks. The most common limits are 52 weeks and eight weeks, each appearing in 16 percent of limitations. Following in frequency are limitations of 10 weeks (10 percent) and 4 weeks (6 percent).

## Income Maintenance Provisions

*(Frequency Expressed as Percentage of Industry Contracts)*

| | Income Maintenance Provision | Work or Pay Guarantee | Severance | SUB * |
|---|---|---|---|---|
| ALL INDUSTRIES | 52 | 13 | 40 | 14 |
| MANUFACTURING | 54 | 6 | 45 | 13 |
| Apparel | — | — | — | — |
| Chemicals | 69 | — | 69 | — |
| Electrical Machinery | 65 | — | 65 | 25 |
| Fabricated Metals | 42 | — | 32 | 21 |
| Foods | 90 | 33 | 86 | 10 |
| Furniture | 17 | — | 17 | — |
| Leather | 50 | — | 50 | — |
| Lumber | — | — | — | — |
| Machinery | 54 | — | 50 | 31 |
| Paper | 57 | — | 57 | — |
| Petroleum | 57 | — | 57 | — |
| Primary Metals | 60 | — | 40 | 52 |
| Printing | 88 | 38 | 63 | — |
| Rubber | 50 | — | 50 | 33 |
| Stone-Clay-Glass | 31 | — | 31 | 15 |
| Textiles | 20 | 10 | 10 | — |
| Transportation Equipment | 62 | 12 | 32 | 50 |
| NON-MANUFACTURING | 50 | 23 | 33 | 1 |
| Communications | 100 | — | 100 | — |
| Construction | 7 | 3 | 3 | 3 |
| Insurance & Finance | 57 | 14 | 43 | — |
| Maritime | 63 | 50 | 13 | 13 |
| Mining | 42 | — | 33 | 8 |
| Retail | 78 | 44 | 52 | 4 |
| Services | 37 | 19 | 19 | — |
| Transportation | 68 | 44 | 44 | — |
| Utilities | 30 | 20 | 20 | — |

* Includes plans not available for analysis in this study.

A minimum service requirement is found in 84 percent of severance pay plans. One year of service is called for by 44 percent of minimum service provisions; two years by 16 percent; three years by 16 percent; six months by 7 percent; five years by 7 percent.

Restrictions on receipt of benefits are imposed in 60 percent of severance pay plans. Forty percent of these clauses deny benefits if employees refuse other work; another 40 percent deny benefits to employees if they are eligible for pensions. More than one-third (39 percent) of agreements placing limitations on receipt of benefits state that workers who quit are ineligible for severance pay. Benefits are denied for various other reasons under 69 percent of these restrictions.

Reemployment after receipt of severance benefits is mentioned in 40 percent of plans studied. Nineteen percent of provisions discussing reemployment after severance state that repayment of severance benefits is not required. Almost one-third (31 percent) of these clauses state that seniority earned before layoff will not be reinstated.

Financing is discussed—often under SUB financing provisions—in 13 percent of severance pay plans. Of severance provisions mentioning financing, 91 percent require the company to bear all costs, and 62 percent place some limit on the company's obligation.

*Industry pattern:* Severance pay provisions appear in every agreement in communications and in at least half of contracts in chemicals, electrical machinery, foods, leather, machinery, paper, petroleum, printing, retail, and rubber. Severance provisions are absent from all surveyed agreements in apparel, and lumber and are found in only one contract each in construction, furniture, maritime and textiles.

## Supplemental Unemployment Benefits

Fifty-seven of the 400 sample contracts make some reference to supplemental unemployment benefit plans. In this study, all such plans are referred to as SUB plans. No text or descriptive material is available for 25 of these plans. Therefore, the working sample in the following analysis consists of 32 plans for which sufficient detail was available.

SUB plans fall into two categories: pooled fund systems and individual account plans. Pooled fund systems provide benefits only in the event of lack of work. Under individual account plans, employees have a vested right to their accounts and may withdraw the full amount at termination. Individual account plans sometimes impose a maximum for each account and limit the amount employees may withdraw each week. Some of these plans allow employees to withdraw money from the account for reasons other than layoff and termination. Only seven individual account plans appear in the present study.

*Industry pattern:* Of the 57 SUB plans (including those that were unavailable), 17 are in transportation equipment, 13 in primary metals, and eight in machinery. Five plans are in electrical machinery, and four in fabricated metals. Two plans each are found in foods and rubber, and one each appears in construction, maritime, mining, retail, and stone-clay-glass.

## Income Maintenance Provisions, By Region

*(Frequency Expressed as Percentage of Contracts in Each Region)*

| | Income Maintenance Provision | Work or Pay Guarantee | Severance | SUB* |
|---|---|---|---|---|
| Middle Atlantic | 53 | 12 | 45 | 6 |
| Midwest | 42 | 13 | 33 | 4 |
| Northeast | 44 | 12 | 28 | 8 |
| North Central | 51 | 10 | 41 | 9 |
| Rocky Mountain | 50 | 30 | 30 | 0 |
| Southeast | 48 | 8 | 40 | 12 |
| Southwest | 39 | 8 | 31 | 8 |
| West Coast | 41 | 17 | 20 | 9 |
| Multiregion | 77 | 16 | 60 | 42 |

* Includes plans not available for analysis in this study.

Among unions in the sample that negotiated SUB plans were the United Auto Workers with 20 plans in the sample and the United Steelworkers with 14 plans. The International Association of Machinists and the International Union of Electronic Workers each agreed to four plans. The Allied Industrial Workers, Bakery, Confectionery, and Tobacco Workers, United Rubber Workers, and Seafarers' International Union were party to two plans each. The other unions in the sample—each represented by one plan—are the Aluminum, Brick and Glass Workers; International Brotherhood of Electrical Workers; United Electrical Workers; Food and Commercial Workers; Metal Trades Council; International Union of Operating Engineers; Plumbers; and Independent Steel Workers Union.

*Full week benefits* are computed by a variety of methods. The most common method of computation, found in ten plans, is payment of an amount equal to a percentage of an employee's take-home pay, with the amount of weekly unemployment compensation (UC) usually deducted. Eight of these provisions (mostly plans in transportation equipment or machinery) pay an amount which, when added to an employee's unemployment compensation, equals 95 percent of take-home pay minus $7.50, $12.50, or $17.50 in work-related expenses not incurred. The percentage of take-home home pay in the other two plans ranges from 65 to 85 percent.

The next most common computation method, payment of a multiple of an employee's hourly rate (usually minus UC), occurs in 9 plans and is found most often in primary metals. Four of these pay 26 times an employee's hourly rate, one pays a multiple of 20, three pay multiples of 28, and one pays a multiple of 37.5.

Five SUB plans pay a percentage of straight time pay (minus UC). Two electrical machinery industry plans pay 60 percent of straight time pay, one plan in machinery pays 62 percent, one in transportation equipment pays 70 percent, and one in rubber pays 80 percent. Other methods of calculating payment include a percentage of an employee's individual account and various amounts based on an employee's job classification.

In most plans that describe the amount of full-week benefits, the amount is affected by receipt of unemployment compensation.

*Maximum payments* are specified in 19 plans. Six of these plans state a flat weekly maximum. These maximums are: $50, $60, $90, $150, $260, and $336.

Five plans (mostly in primary metals) provide two maximums: one for weeks in which employees receive UC benefits and one for weeks in which they do not. These two maximums are $50 and $75 in one plan, $150 and $200 in one, and $180 and $235 in three. Maximum ranges were unchanged from the previous study.

Seven plans (mostly in transportation equipment) state a maximum only for weeks in which an employee is no longer receiving UC and/or has refused an offer of work. The maximum is $50 in one plan, $115 in three, $135 in two, and $150 in one.

*Minimum payments* are specified in 12 plans analyzed. In two-thirds of these, $2 is the minimum payment. Following in frequency are minimum ranges of $3 to $258.

Dependents' allowances are added to full-week benefits in 6 plans (mostly in primary metals). The amount is $1.50 per dependent under all of the plans. All plans limit amounts added to four dependents.

*Duration of benefits* is discussed in 27 plans. A majority (78 percent) of these cancel credit units for each week an employee receives benefits; others link duration directly to seniority (52 percent) and/or to the condition of the trust fund (44 percent). In plans using credit units, employees generally accrue a specified number of credit units per week or per pay period, up to a maximum. When an employee begins to collect benefits, credit units are cancelled. The number of credit units cancelled per benefit often depends on the condition of the SUB trust fund and an employee's seniority.

A typical plan using credit units states that an employee, after attaining one year of seniority, will accure one-half credit unit per week up to a maximum of 52 credit units. When an employee begins to draw benefits, the number of credit units cancelled per benefit depends on the condition of the trust fund. When the fund is at its highest level, one credit unit per benefit is cancelled, regardless of seniority—thus the maximum is computed as 52 weeks. When fund levels drop, a greater number of credit units are cancelled per benefit, depending on seniority. As many as 10 credit units per benefit may be cancelled for employees with limited seniority when a fund reaches a low level. When funds drop below a specified level, benefit payments cease completely.

Some plans basing duration on credit units cancel a fixed number of credit units per benefit but reduce the amount of benefit when a trust fund falls below a certain level.

A maximum duration is stated in 25 plans. Under 10 plans, the maximum is 52 weeks. A 104-week maximum is provided under eight plans. Maximums are 39 weeks, and five years in each of two plans. Other maximums, appearing in only one agreement each, are 20 weeks, 27 weeks, and four years. In most cases maximums of more than 52 weeks apply only to workers with long service.

*Seniority requirements* for SUB eligibility are found in 26 plans. One year is the requirement in 14 plans, and two years is specified in 11 plans. The remaining plan requires five years' seniority.

Most of the plans studied deny payment of SUB for layoffs of a disciplinary nature (25 contracts), those resulting from a labor dispute (27 contracts), or those caused by circumstances beyond an employer's control such as a civil riot or natural disaster (19 contracts).

*Employee obligations* that have become a standard part of most SUB plans include the following: an employee must apply for benefits (23 agreements); accept company offer of other work (16 plans); accept suitable work offered by the state unemployment service (17 agreements); receive or be eligible to receive unemployment compensation (25 agreements). In over half the available plans, an employee is required to accept a company work offer.

Of the 25 plans requiring an employee to receive or be eligible to receive unemployment compensation, 22 state exceptions to this rule. Exceptions include: exhaustion of UC rights (22 plans); an insufficient period of work under a state system to qualify for a benefit (20 plans); a second waiting week under a state system (15 plans); receipt of other compensation disqualifying an employee for UC benefits (20 plans); receipt of disability or retirement benefits an employee could have received while at work (11 plans); a benefit denial contrary to the intent of the plan; rejection of a company work offer as allowed by the contract; or participation in a federal training program (9 plans each). Other exceptions are found in 17 plans.

*Short workweek benefits* are available under 18 of the SUB plans. In 10 of these provisions, payment is based on numbers of hours worked under 40 and in the remainder, on hours worked under 32. Benefits are computed as the number of unworked hours times 80 percent of straight-time pay in eight of the provisions, and times 100 percent in another eight of the provisions. Under the remaining two of these clauses, the amount paid varies according to seniority. Eligibility requirements generally are the same as for full-week benefits, and all plans state that short workweek benefits will be paid automatically without employee application.

Financing is mentioned in 21 of sample pooled-fund plans. In all of these plans an employer contributes a certain amount per hour worked; in 19 an employer's obligation ceases after the SUB fund reaches a specific maximum.

---

# 7

## Hours and Overtime

Hours and overtime provisions are found in all but two of the 400 contracts in CBNC's Basic Patterns database. All manufacturing contracts contain these provisions. In non-manufacturing, two insurance and finance agreements omit them. Geographic analysis of the sample shows hours and overtime provisions appear in all contracts in all regions except multiregion (97 percent).

Typical provisions include daily and weekly work schedules, requirements for overtime premiums, regulations for the distribution of overtime work, length of lunch and rest periods, and rules governing pay for time lost on a day of injury or for time spent traveling to and from work.

### Work Schedules

*Daily work schedules* are specified in 85 percent of contracts studied. Of these, 95 percent call for an eight-hour day and 5 percent provide for a standard workday of less than eight hours. Two contracts call for workdays of more than eight hours.

*Industry pattern:* Less than eight-hour workdays are specified in 4 percent of manufacturing and in 5 percent of non-manufacturing industry agreements. These provisions predominate only in printing with all but one contract specifying a daily work schedule of seven and one-half hours or less.

*Weekly work schedules* are spelled out in 61 percent of the sample. Of these, the majority (93 percent) provide a normal workweek of 40 hours; the remainder specify workweeks ranging from 35 to 37.5 hours.

*Industry pattern:* Provisions for less than 40-hour workweeks appear in 4 percent of manufacturing and and in 5 percent of non-manufacturing agreements. Shorter workweeks are specified in 78 percent of apparel agreements; the remainder are scattered throughout the sample.

*Five-day workweeks* are specified in 54 percent of contracts; 39 percent of sample contracts call for a Monday-through-Friday schedule.

### Scheduling of Work

Work scheduling is a management prerogative under 47 percent of contracts included in the database—49 percent in manufacturing and 44 percent in non-manufacturing. Sixty percent of the sample contracts discuss work schedule changes. These provisions appear in 65 percent of manufacturing agreements and 51 percent of non-manufacturing contracts. Of the change in work schedules clauses, 41 percent require notification to or discussion with the union; 36 percent require union agreement.

### Overtime Work

Nearly all agreements studied (97 percent) provide premium pay for overtime work. These provisions are found in 99 percent of manufacturing agreements and in 94 percent of non-manufacturing contracts.

*Daily overtime premiums* are provided in 94 percent of agreements. Of these, 85 percent require overtime pay after eight hours' work and 4 percent provide premium pay after less than eight hours. Provisions calling for overtime premiums after seven or seven and one-half hours' work predominate in printing and apparel agreements. Work before or after the regular daily schedule is paid at the overtime rate under 25 percent of sample contracts.

*Daily overtime rates* are specified in 92 percent of agreements. Nearly all of these provisions call for time and one-half; two call for doubletime.

Under 27 percent of sample agreements, a doubletime premium is paid after a specified number of hours beyond the daily schedule have been worked at a time and one-half rate. This type of premium pay appears more frequently in manufacturing contracts (29 percent) than in non-manufacturing contracts (23 percent). Of these clauses, 58 percent pay doubletime after four hours of overtime work; 19 percent after two hours; and 12 percent after eight hours.

*Weekly overtime pay provisions* are stipulated in 69 percent of agreements—70 percent in manufacturing and 67 percent in non-manufacturing. Of these, 94 percent pay time and one-half after 40 hours' work, while 5 percent pay overtime for less than 40 hours' work (mainly in the apparel industry).

*Sixth-day premiums* are called for in 22 percent of contracts—25 percent in manufacturing and 18 percent in non-manufacturing. All of these agreements provide time and one-half pay for work on the sixth day. A requirement that the sixth day be the sixth consecutive day of work in order to qualify for overtime pay is found in 38 percent of the clauses.

*Seventh-day premiums* are paid in 26 percent of contracts—32 percent in manufacturing and 17 percent in non-manufacturing. Of these provisions, 87 percent call for doubletime rates and 58 percent contain a consecutive day" requirement.

*Layoffs to avoid weekly overtime* are prohibited under 24 percent of agreements—24 percent in manufacturing and 24 percent in non-manufacturing. These prohibitions are found in 75 percent of mining, 71 percent each of paper and petroleum, and 50 percent or more of lumber, chemicals, stone-clay-glass, and utilities agreements.

*Pyramiding of overtime pay* is prohibited in 66 percent of contracts in the database—75 percent in manufacturing and 51 percent in non-manufacturing. Under such provisions, neither payment of both daily and weekly overtime for the same hours of work nor more than one type of premium for any one day (holiday pay plus doubletime on seventh day worked, for example) is allowed. In 21 of the 26 industries studied, at least half of the agreements contain pyramiding provisions.

# Hours and Overtime Provisions

*(Frequency Expressed as Percentage of Contracts in Each Region)*

| | All Regions | Middle Atlantic | Midwest | New England | North Central | Rocky Mountain | Southeast | Southwest | West Coast | Multiregion |
|---|---|---|---|---|---|---|---|---|---|---|
| Work Schedule Provisions | 96 | 99 | 100 | 96 | 97 | 100 | 98 | 92 | 98 | 85 |
| **Schedule Specified** | | | | | | | | | | |
| Daily | 85 | 83 | 75 | 92 | 87 | 70 | 88 | 100 | 91 | 78 |
| Weekly | 61 | 57 | 67 | 80 | 60 | 70 | 54 | 77 | 72 | 55 |
| Monday thru Friday | 39 | 45 | 42 | 40 | 37 | 20 | 34 | 39 | 48 | 33 |
| Overtime Pay Provisions | 97 | 98 | 96 | 100 | 99 | 100 | 96 | 100 | 98 | 90 |
| **Premium Pay for** | | | | | | | | | | |
| Daily OT | 94 | 94 | 96 | 100 | 98 | 80 | 92 | 100 | 94 | 85 |
| Weekly OT | 69 | 66 | 71 | 76 | 73 | 70 | 86 | 69 | 59 | 55 |
| Sixth Day OT | 22 | 22 | 38 | 12 | 19 | 20 | 26 | 8 | 24 | 23 |
| Seventh Day OT | 26 | 24 | 33 | 16 | 23 | — | 42 | 15 | 26 | 30 |
| Saturday OT | 51 | 53 | 54 | 60 | 71 | 30 | 32 | 31 | 46 | 38 |
| Sunday OT | 65 | 64 | 67 | 84 | 82 | 60 | 50 | 62 | 57 | 55 |
| Layoffs to Avoid Prohibited | 24 | 23 | 8 | 20 | 26 | 20 | 34 | 39 | 15 | 28 |
| Pyramiding Prohibited | 66 | 66 | 67 | 76 | 70 | 50 | 80 | 54 | 46 | 62 |
| Advance Notice Required | 26 | 30 | 29 | 16 | 35 | 10 | 14 | 0 | 17 | 37 |
| Distribution Procedures | 63 | 65 | 63 | 52 | 81 | 30 | 66 | 69 | 41 | 58 |

***Distribution of overtime work*** is discussed in 67 percent of the sample—78 percent of manufacturing agreements and 48 percent of non-manufacturing contracts. A general statement to the effect that overtime will be equally distributed as far as practical or possible is contained in 67 percent of distribution provisions.

Procedures for the distribution of overtime work are defined in 63 percent of the sample and are far more common in manufacturing (74 percent) than in non-manufacturing (47 percent) contracts. Of the distribution clauses, 34 percent spread overtime equally among all employees; 17 percent assign overtime on a strict seniority basis; 12 percent provide for cumulative equalization of overtime; and 9 percent distribute overtime by rotating assignments.

Of the agreements containing overtime distribution procedures, 57 percent limit assignments to employees within a job classification; 48 percent to employees within a department; 29 percent to employees qualified to do the job; and 26 percent each percent to employees who normally perform the work and to employees on a particular shift.

Overtime records are required to be posted under 18 percent of agreements. Records must be made available to the union under 19 percent of the contracts analyzed. Seven percent of sample contracts specify that disputes over distribution of overtime are subject to the grievance procedure.

*Acceptance of overtime work* is discussed in 23 percent of the 400 agreements. In 45 percent of these provisions, overtime is mandatory; in 42 percent it is voluntary; in 13 percent it is voluntary except in case of emergency. Of the 22 percent of contracts imposing penalties for refusal of overtime work, nearly all (92 percent) specify a loss of claim to the number of hours refused. A penalty for not reporting for accepted overtime is contained in 9 percent of the sample.

*Restrictions on overtime assignments* are imposed in 37 percent of sample contracts—48 percent in manufacturing and 20 percent in non-manufacturing. Under 70 percent of these provisions, advance notice (or advance notice except in case of emergency) of overtime assignments is required. Failure to give advance notice relieves employees of the obligation to work overtime under 13 percent of agreements discussing restrictions. Overtime is prohibited during periods of layoff in 7 percent of contracts containing restrictions, and a maximum is placed on the amount of overtime allowed in 25 percent.

## Premium Pay for Weekend Work

A premium rate is paid for weekend work under 67 percent of sample contracts in the database. Weekend premiums are provided in 78 percent of manufacturing agreements and 48 percent of non-manufacturing agreements.

*Premium pay for work on Saturday* as such is provided in 51 percent of contracts. The standard premium rate is time and one-half, although 12 percent of the sample pays doubletime after a given number of hours' work (most often eight). Less than 2 percent of agreements specifying Saturday premiums provide for doubletime for all Saturday work. In construction, where this practice was most common, the frequency of doubletime for all Saturday work in agreements containing Saturday premiums dropped from 52 percent in the 1979 analysis to 38 percent in 1983, to 7 percent in 1986, and to zero in this study.

*Industry pattern:* Saturday premiums are found in more than twice the percentage of manufacturing (64 percent) contracts as in non-manufacturing (30 percent) contracts. Such provisions appear most frequently in machinery (92 percent), electrical machinery (90 percent), fabricated metal (89 percent), construction (83 percent), and transportation equipment (82 percent) agreements.

*Premium pay for work on Sunday* as such is required in 65 percent of contracts. Doubletime pay, the most common premium for Sunday work, is provided under 78 percent of these agreements; 21 percent pay time and one-half. Two of these provisions call for time and one-quarter, and one calls for tripletime.

*Industry pattern:* Sunday premiums are paid under 78 percent of manufacturing agreements and 46 percent of non-manufacturing agreements. They are found in all leather, furniture, and rubber contracts; in 96 percent of machinery contracts; in 93 percent of paper agreements; in 90 percent each of electrical machinery and construction contracts; and in more than three-fourths of those in stone-clay-glass, transportation equipment, textiles, and fabricated metals industries.

Of sample contracts specifying premium pay for Sunday work, doubletime prevails in chemicals, construction, electrical machinery, fabricated metals, furniture, insurance and finance, machinery, textiles, rubber, and transportation equipment.

## Lunch, Rest, and Cleanup Provisions

*Lunch periods* are referred to in 61 percent of the sample contracts. Such provisions appear in 51 percent of manufacturing and 76 percent of non-manufacturing contracts. Of the 53 percent of sample agreements specifying the amount of time allowed, 64 percent grant half-hour lunch periods and 22 percent provide an hour.

Twenty-four percent of contracts provide paid lunch periods; two-thirds of these pay only under certain conditions.

Provisions for working through the regular lunch period are found in 21 percent of the sample. Twenty-three percent of these clauses call for regular pay. Of the 16 percent of contracts that provide overtime pay, 34 percent grant overtime pay only after a certain number of hours without lunch.

### Lunch-Time Provisions
*(Frequency Expressed as Percentage of Contracts\*)*

|  | Lunch Time | Amount of Time | Less than 30 mins. | 30 mins. | 31-59 mins. | One Hour |
|---|---|---|---|---|---|---|
| All Industries | 61 | 53 | 7 | 34 | * | 12 |
| Manufacturing | 51 | 44 | 9 | 29 | * | 6 |
| Non-manufacturing | 76 | 66 | 3 | 41 | 1 | 21 |

\* Less than 1 percent

*Meals during overtime hours* are mentioned in 32 percent of agreements surveyed. Under contracts detailing meal provisions, 29 percent call for a paid lunch period; 25 percent pay a meal allowance; 13 percent call for a company-furnished meal; 15 percent provide the option of an allowance or a meal furnished by the company; and 11 percent provide for a paid lunch period and a meal furnished by the company.

Seven percent of clauses dealing with overtime meals restrict this provision to employees who are not given advance notice of overtime.

Usually an overtime meal or allowance is called for only after a specified number of hours of overtime (although a few contracts specify work to a certain hour); this is true in 30 percent of agreements in the database. While overtime requirements range from one to seven and one-half hours, the most common requirements found in contracts containing such provisions are two hours (64 percent) and three and four hours (each 10 percent). Forty-one percent of contracts dealing with overtime meal requirements call for a second meal or allowance after an additional period of overtime work. Of these, 59 percent require four hours of overtime; 24 percent require five hours; and 8 percent require six hours.

*Industry pattern:* Clauses concerning overtime meals appear in 27 percent of manufacturing contracts and in 38 percent of non-manufacturing contracts. Ninety-two percent of mining, 90 percent of utilities, 86 percent of petroleum, and 81 percent of chemical industry agreements contain this provision. At least a third of contracts in foods, paper, printing, construction, transportation, maritime, and communications contain overtime meal provisions.

**Rest periods** are referred to in 44 percent of agreements. Of these, 11 percent merely state that rest periods will be allowed according to plant or past practice, and 25 percent provide additional breaks during overtime hours. Under contracts containing details on rest periods, 88 percent provide two breaks per shift. Of agreements specifying the amount of time allowed, 57 percent provide 10-minute breaks, and 36 percent provide 15-minute breaks.

*Industry pattern:* Rest periods are referred to in 42 percent of manufacturing agreements and in 48 percent of non-manufacturing agreements. Such provisions are found in one-half or more of leather, paper, furniture, communications, retail, foods, rubber, services, fabricated metals, chemicals, insurance and finance, and maritime contracts.

**Time to clean up and prepare for or cease work** is considered in 21 percent of contracts—25 percent in manufacturing and 15 percent in non-manufacturing. Of agreements containing such provisions, 61 percent provide for personal washup time and 16 percent for clothes-changing time. Thirty-eight percent of the provisions grant time for returning tools, checking equipment, or filing required reports. In contracts stating the amount of time allowed, 41 percent specify five minutes, and 36 percent specify 10 minutes. Such provisions are most common in furniture (50 percent), transportation (40 percent), petroleum (43 percent), and chemicals (56 percent) agreements.

## Other Non-productive Time

**Payment for time lost on a day of injury** is provided for in 44 percent of the sample contracts. This provision appears in 50 percent of manufacturing and 33 percent of non-manufacturing contracts. Typical clauses state that an employee leaving work because of an injury shall receive a full day's pay, regardless of the time of the injury. All rubber and more than 50 percent of machinery, primary metals, foods, paper, fabricated metals, transportation equipment, and mining contracts provide pay for time lost on the day of injury.

## Overtime Provisions

*(Frequency Expressed as Percentage of Contracts in Each Industry)*

| | Provisions | Daily OT | Weekly OT | 6th Day OT | 7th Day OT | Saturday OT | Sunday OT | Layoffs to Avoid Prohibited | Pyramiding Prohibited | Advance Notice Required | Distribution Procedures |
|---|---|---|---|---|---|---|---|---|---|---|---|
| | | | | *PREMIUM PAY FOR* | | | | | | | |
| ALL INDUSTRIES | 97 | 94 | 69 | 22 | 26 | 51 | 65 | 24 | 66 | 26 | 63 |
| MANUFACTURING | 99 | 96 | 70 | 25 | 32 | 64 | 78 | 25 | 75 | 36 | 74 |
| Apparel | 100 | 100 | 33 | 11 | 22 | 44 | 33 | — | 33 | 67 | 44 |
| Chemicals | 100 | 100 | 94 | 38 | 69 | 50 | 63 | 50 | 100 | — | 88 |
| Elec. Machinery | 100 | 100 | 50 | 25 | 30 | 90 | 90 | 10 | 60 | 40 | 80 |
| Fab. Metals | 100 | 100 | 79 | 16 | 16 | 89 | 84 | 16 | 79 | 47 | 89 |
| Food | 100 | 90 | 86 | 24 | 29 | 62 | 67 | 24 | 71 | 19 | 62 |
| Furniture | 100 | 100 | 67 | 17 | 33 | 67 | 100 | 17 | 83 | 67 | 67 |
| Leather | 100 | 100 | 75 | 25 | 25 | 75 | 100 | — | 75 | 25 | 50 |
| Lumber | 100 | 86 | 100 | 14 | 29 | 29 | 43 | 57 | 71 | 29 | 71 |
| Machinery | 100 | 100 | 54 | 23 | 23 | 92 | 96 | 15 | 81 | 27 | 88 |
| Paper | 100 | 100 | 86 | 7 | — | 36 | 93 | 71 | 93 | 14 | 64 |
| Petroleum | 100 | 100 | 86 | 14 | 57 | — | 43 | 71 | 86 | 29 | 86 |
| Primary Metals | 100 | 96 | 80 | 52 | 56 | 52 | 72 | 32 | 84 | 20 | 64 |
| Printing | 75 | 75 | 25 | 13 | 13 | 50 | 50 | — | 13 | 13 | 25 |
| Rubber | 100 | 100 | 67 | 17 | — | 50 | 100 | 17 | 100 | — | 83 |
| Stone, Clay, & Glass | 100 | 100 | 85 | 15 | 46 | 31 | 77 | 54 | 85 | 8 | 54 |
| Textiles | 100 | 100 | 70 | 40 | 50 | 60 | 80 | — | 90 | — | 70 |
| Trans. Equip. | 97 | 91 | 59 | 24 | 29 | 82 | 85 | 6 | 62 | 24 | 91 |
| NON-MANUFACTURING | 94 | 89 | 67 | 18 | 17 | 30 | 46 | 24 | 51 | 11 | 47 |
| Communications | 90 | 90 | 80 | 10 | 10 | 20 | 60 | 20 | 70 | 30 | 80 |
| Construction | 97 | 97 | 38 | — | — | 83 | 90 | 3 | 7 | 3 | 17 |
| Insurance & Finance | 71 | 57 | 57 | — | — | 57 | 57 | — | 29 | — | 43 |
| Maritime | 88 | 75 | — | — | — | 50 | 50 | — | 25 | — | 25 |
| Mining | 100 | 92 | 100 | 25 | 42 | 17 | 17 | 75 | 83 | 8 | 83 |
| Retail | 96 | 96 | 89 | 41 | 19 | 15 | 63 | 22 | 59 | 4 | 41 |
| Services | 96 | 85 | 93 | 37 | 44 | 15 | 19 | 30 | 70 | 11 | 44 |
| Transportation | 88 | 84 | 48 | 8 | 8 | 4 | 8 | 24 | 56 | 4 | 48 |
| Utilities | 100 | 100 | 80 | 10 | 10 | 10 | 50 | 50 | 70 | — | 90 |

*Waiting time* —time spent while waiting for work or materials—is considered in 19 percent of the sample (20 percent in manufacturing and 17 percent in non-manufacturing). Of these provisions, 88 percent provide full pay for waiting time; the remainder provide less than full pay. Waiting time provisions appear most frequently in leather (75 percent), rubber (67 percent), apparel (56 percent), transportation (52 percent), and textiles (50 percent) contracts.

*Standby time* (time spent at home but on call) provisions are found in 4 percent of the sample, appearing in 2 percent of manufacturing agreements and 7 percent of non-manufacturing agreements. Fifty-three percent of these provisions call for full pay; the remainder for less than full pay.

*Travel time* pay of one type or another is provided in 22 percent of agreements. Such provisions appear in a greater proportion of contracts in non-manufacturing industries (41 percent) than in manufacturing (10 percent). Although there is some overlapping in types of paid travel time, usually they fall into one or more of the following categories: portal-to-portal; when called in to work outside of regular work hours; when traveling outside a specified area; and when traveling away from a home office or headquarters. Such provisions are found in all communications and in one-half or more of transportation, maritime, and utilities contracts; the rest are scattered throughout the sample.

*Voting time* (required by law in many states) is mentioned in 7 percent of agreements. Of these, 73 percent provide time off with pay, 15 percent call for time off without pay, and 12 percent state that time off will be given as required by state law.

*Negotiating time* pay (including a requirement that negotiations be held during work hours) is included in 9 percent of the agreements studied—13 percent in manufacturing and 3 percent in non-manufacturing agreements.

# 8

# Holidays

Holidays are provided in 99 percent of contracts included in the basic patterns database sample. All or some of these holidays are observed without loss of pay in 90 percent of agreements.

Geographic analysis of the database shows that contracts calling for a bare bones schedule of seven and one-half or fewer holidays are concentrated in the Rocky Mountain region (40 percent); contracts calling for an ample schedule of 12 or more holidays predominate in the North Central region (42 percent).

Ten or more holidays are found in just under three quarters of agreements, having risen in frequency from 7 percent in 1966 to 71 percent in the present survey. The number of contracts providing 12 or more holidays also has risen sharply, climbing from 3 percent in 1971 to 31 percent in this study. Fourteen or more holidays are called for in 9 percent of contracts.

## Number of Holidays

The median number of holidays provided in the total sample is 11, the same as in the previous study. Five contracts with holiday provisions provide only five holidays (the lowest number in the sample), while one contract calls for 17 (the highest).

### Number of Holidays Provided

*(Frequency Expressed as Percentage of Contracts)*

| | 6-6½ | 7-7½ | 8-8½ | 9-9½ | 10-10½ | 11-11½ | 12-12½ | 13 or more |
|---|---|---|---|---|---|---|---|---|
| All Industries | 4 | 4 | 8 | 11 | 18 | 22 | 14 | 18 |
| Manufacturing | — | 2 | 4 | 7 | 20 | 27 | 16 | 23 |
| Non-manufacturing | 8 | 8 | 14 | 17 | 15 | 15 | 10 | 9 |

In non-manufacturing the median number of holidays is 9.5 and in manufacturing the median is 11. Ten or more holidays are provided in 85 percent of manufacturing agreements, compared with 48 percent of non-manufacturing agreements. Fewer than 10 holidays are found in 48 percent of non-manufacturing contracts and in only 15 percent of manufacturing agreements.

## Trend in Number of Holidays

*(Frequency Expressed as Percentage of Contracts)*

|  | 1957 | 1961 | 1966 | 1971 | 1975 | 1979 | 1983 | 1986 | 1989 |
|---|---|---|---|---|---|---|---|---|---|
| None specified | 1 | 1 | 1 | 1 | 1 | 2 | 2 | 2 | 1 |
| Fewer than 7 | 36 | 22 | 16 | 11 | 6 | 4 | 3 | 3 | 5 |
| 7-7½ | 43 | 47 | 39 | 15 | 10 | 8 | 5 | 6 | 4 |
| 8-8½ | 12 | 23 | 31 | 25 | 12 | 11 | 8 | 8 | 8 |
| 9-9½ | 4 | 5 | 7 | 27 | 29 | 17 | 11 | 9 | 11 |
| 10-10½ | 4 | 5* | 7* | 16 | 20 | 27 | 23 | 23 | 18 |
| 11-11½ | — | — | — | 4 | 12 | 15 | 20 | 18 | 22 |
| 12-12½ | — | — | — | 3** | 10** | 11 | 13 | 14 | 14 |
| 13 or more | — | — | — | — | — | 6 | 16 | 19 | 18 |

*10 or more.
**12 or more.

*Industry pattern:* All manufacturing contracts in the sample provide some holidays. In non-manufacturing, 97 percent of agreements contain a holiday clause, the exceptions being three contracts in transportation and one in insurance and finance. In addition, two contracts with holiday provisions—one each in mining and services—do not state which holidays are observed.

In eight of the 26 industries studied—furniture, leather, lumber, mining, petroleum, primary metals, printing, and transportation—the median number of holidays is 10. The median is 11 in apparel, chemicals, electrical machinery, fabricated metals, foods, rubber and stone-clay-glass. The lowest median is seven in construction; the highest is 13 in transportation equipment.

In the remaining industries, medians are 8 in services, 9 in retail and textiles, 10.5 in utilities, 11.5 in communications and insurance and finance, 12 each in machinery and paper, and 12.75 in maritime.

## Number of Holidays, By Region

*(Frequency Expressed as Percentage of Contracts in Each Region)*

|  | 5-5½ | 6-6½ | 7-7½ | 8-8½ | 9-9½ | 10-10½ | 11-11½ | 12-12½ | 13 or more |
|---|---|---|---|---|---|---|---|---|---|
| Middle Atlantic | 1 | 1 | 2 | 5 | 11 | 17 | 23 | 17 | 22 |
| Midwest | — | 8 | 13 | 4 | 13 | 17 | 21 | 17 | 8 |
| Northeast | — | — | 8 | — | 16 | 8 | 28 | 20 | 20 |
| North Central | — | 5 | 3 | 5 | 5 | 16 | 26 | 16 | 26 |
| Rocky Mountain | — | 30 | 10 | 10 | — | 30 | 20 | — | — |
| Southeast | 4 | — | 10 | 12 | 18 | 26 | 16 | 2 | 12 |
| Southwest | — | 8 | 8 | 8 | 31 | 15 | 15 | 8 | 8 |
| West Coast | — | — | — | 28 | 15 | 13 | 22 | 15 | 7 |
| Multiregion | 2 | 2 | 3 | 3 | 5 | 32 | 17 | 13 | 17 |

## Days Observed as Holidays

Thanksgiving and Christmas Day each are observed in all but three contracts specifying holidays, Labor Day in all but four, Independence Day in all but seven, New Year's Day in all but eight, and Memorial Day in all but 18. These six traditional holidays appear as a group in 91 percent of sample contracts.

Following in frequency are two holidays found in slightly more than half of agreements analyzed: the day after Thanksgiving (58 percent) and Christmas Eve as a full or half holiday (52 percent).

Good Friday is designated as a holiday in 48 percent of sample contracts, Washington's Birthday is specified in 33 percent, New Year's Eve appears in 29 percent, an employee's birthday is observed in 22 percent, Veterans' Day is found in 17 percent, and floating holidays are provided in 16 percent.

*Martin Luther King's Birthday* (14 percent) and personal days (18 percent) showed the most growth among contractual holidays, rising 5 percent and 2 percent respectively, from the last survey. Regionally, Martin Luther King's birthday appears most frequently in West Coast and Middle Atlantic States contracts. Other less celebrated holidays include Columbus Day (9 percent); Election Day (8 percent); one or more days between Christmas and New Year's (8 percent), Easter Monday (4 percent); one or more days chosen locally (4 percent); Lincoln's Birthday (3 percent); and the eves of Christmas and New Year's as half holidays (2 percent each).

Holidays other than those listed above are found in 27 percent of the sample. Among these are extra personal time or floating days, the day before or after another holiday to provide a long weekend, Easter Sunday, a "bonus" day, an employee's anniversary date of employment, Yom Kippur, Rosh Hashanah, Flag Day, Inauguration Day, May Day, and days of local or regional significance such as Patriot's Day, Mardi Gras Day, and Pioneer Day. In 9 percent of contracts, days observed vary from year to year.

*Industry pattern:* Extra time off during the Christmas season and days such as the Friday after Thanksgiving to stretch a holiday into a long weekend are more often found in manufacturing contracts than in non-manufacturing. Floating days and days observed on varying dates from year to year also are more prevalent in manufacturing.

In non-manufacturing industries, on the other hand, extra time to create long weekends is avoided, and holidays such as Washington's Birthday, Veterans' Day, Columbus Day, and Lincoln's Birthday are more common. Individualized holidays such as personal time and employee birthdays also prevail in non-manufacturing.

## Most Commonly Observed Holidays

*(Frequency Expressed as Percentage of Contracts)*

| Holiday | All Industries | Manu-facturing | Non-manu-facturing |
|---|---|---|---|
| Thanksgiving | 98 | 99 | 97 |
| Labor Day | 98 | 100 | 95 |
| Christmas | 98 | 99 | 97 |
| Independence Day | 97 | 98 | 96 |
| New Year's Day | 97 | 98 | 95 |
| Memorial Day | 94 | 95 | 94 |
| Day after Thanksgiving | 58 | 78 | 28 |
| Good Friday, including ½ day | 48 | 67 | 19 |
| Christmas Eve | 50 | 69 | 20 |
| Washington's Birthday | 33 | 28 | 41 |
| New Year's Eve | 29 | 43 | 7 |
| Employee's birthday | 22 | 16 | 32 |
| Personal day | 22 | 11 | 28 |
| Veterans' Day | 17 | 11 | 27 |
| Floating day | 16 | 17 | 13 |
| Martin Luther King's Birthday | 15 | 10 | 20 |
| Christmas-New Year's week | 12 | 19 | — |
| Columbus Day | 9 | 8 | 12 |
| Election day | 8 | 8 | 8 |
| Other days during Christmas week | 8 | 13 | 1 |
| Easter Monday | 4 | 6 | 2 |
| Day chosen locally | 4 | 4 | 4 |
| Lincoln's Birthday | 3 | 1 | 6 |
| Christmas Eve, ½ day | 2 | 1 | 3 |
| New Year's Eve, ½ day | 2 | 1 | 2 |

*The traditional six holidays* are provided in 91 percent of both manufacturing and non-manufacturing contracts. Good Friday as a full or half holiday is far more common in manufacturing (67 percent) than non-manufacturing (19 percent). It is found in three-quarters or more of agreements in apparel, chemicals, electrical machinery, furniture, leather, machinery, petroleum, and primary metals. Utilities is the only non-manufacturing industry in which a majority of contracts provide Good Friday as a holiday.

The day after Thanksgiving is provided in 78 percent of manufacturing agreements and 28 percent of non-manufacturing contracts. Manufacturing industries in which three-quarters or more of contracts provide the day after Thanksgiving as a holiday are chemicals, electrical machinery, fabricated metals, furniture, leather, lumber, machinery, petroleum, primary metals, stone-clay-glass, and transportation equipment. In non-manufacturing it is provided in a majority of communications, insurance and finance, mining, and utilities agreements.

Christmas Eve is observed as a full day in 69 percent of manufacturing agreements and as a half day in 1 percent, compared with 20 percent as a full day and 3 percent as a half day in non-manufacturing agreements. Full or partial observance of Christmas Eve is called for in four-fifths or more of contracts in electrical machinery, fabricated metals, furniture, lumber, and paper. Mining and utilities are the only non-manufacturing industries in which at least half of contracts provide Christmas Eve as a holiday.

New Year's Eve is a full or half holiday in 45 percent of manufacturing contracts, compared with only 9 percent of non-manufacturing agreements. More than 50 percent of contracts in fabricated metals, machinery, primary metals, rubber, and transportation equipment call for this holiday. Observance of the entire Christmas-to-New Year's week is found only in manufacturing. The full week is provided in nearly three-quarters of transportation equipment contracts and almost two-fifths of machinery agreements.

Washington's Birthday is more common in non-manufacturing (41 percent) than manufacturing (28 percent). More than half of sample agreements in apparel, communications, foods, insurance and finance, maritime, petroleum, and utilities provide time off in honor of the first President's birthday.

An employee's birthday, observed in 16 percent of manufacturing contracts and 32 percent of non-manufacturing contracts, is found in at least half of printing, retail, rubber, and transportation agreements. Floating holidays, which appear in 17 percent of manufacturing contracts and 13 percent of non-manufacturing agreements, are provided for in one-quarter to one-half of agreements in chemicals, communications, fabricated metals, furniture, insurance and finance, lumber, paper, petroleum, and services.

Veteran's Day is observed in 11 percent of the manufacturing and 27 percent of the non-manufacturing sample. One-quarter of contracts in leather, four-fifths of agreements in utilities, and all contracts in maritime provide Veteran's Day as a holiday.

Columbus Day appears in 8 percent of manufacturing contracts and 12 percent of non-manufacturing agreements. Observance of Columbus Day is most prevalent in maritime (63 percent) and apparel (56 percent) contracts.

## Holiday Pay

Holiday pay is provided for all recognized holidays in 88 percent of the database sample—97 percent in manufacturing and 74 percent in non-manufacturing. One percent of the sample provides for some paid and some unpaid holidays. Only two agreements, both in construction, state that no pay will be provided for holidays.

## Most Common Holidays by Industry

*(Frequency Expressed as Percentage of Industry Contracts)*

| | New Year's Day | Washington's Birthday | Good Friday (full or ½ day) | Memorial Day | Independence Day | Labor Day | Veterans' Day | Thanksgiving | Day after Thanksgiving | Christmas Eve (full or ½ day) | Christmas | New Year's Eve (full or ½ day) | Employee's birthday | Floating day |
|---|---|---|---|---|---|---|---|---|---|---|---|---|---|---|
| ALL INDUSTRIES | 97 | 33 | 48 | 94 | 97 | 98 | 17 | 98 | 58 | 52 | 98 | 31 | 22 | 16 |
| MANUFACTURING | 98 | 28 | 67 | 95 | 98 | 99 | 11 | 99 | 78 | 70 | 99 | 45 | 16 | 17 |
| Apparel | 100 | 89 | 78 | 100 | 89 | 100 | — | 100 | 56 | 33 | 100 | 11 | 33 | — |
| Chemicals | 100 | 25 | 88 | 100 | 100 | 100 | 19 | 100 | 88 | 69 | 100 | 31 | 13 | 44 |
| Electrical Machinery | 100 | 40 | 85 | 100 | 100 | 100 | 10 | 100 | 80 | 80 | 100 | 50 | 5 | 10 |
| Fabricated Metals | 100 | 16 | 74 | 89 | 100 | 100 | 16 | 100 | 95 | 89 | 100 | 58 | 21 | 26 |
| Foods | 100 | 67 | 52 | 100 | 100 | 100 | 24 | 100 | 57 | 38 | 100 | 24 | 29 | 14 |
| Furniture | 100 | 17 | 83 | 100 | 100 | 100 | 17 | 100 | 100 | 83 | 100 | 50 | 17 | 33 |
| Leather | 75 | 25 | 75 | 100 | 50 | 100 | 25 | 100 | 100 | 75 | 75 | — | — | — |
| Lumber | 100 | 14 | 57 | 86 | 100 | 100 | — | 100 | 86 | 100 | 100 | 43 | 43 | 29 |
| Machinery | 96 | 15 | 85 | 100 | 100 | 96 | 4 | 100 | 96 | 77 | 96 | 69 | 12 | 15 |
| Paper | 79 | — | 43 | 79 | 100 | 100 | 7 | 86 | 43 | 93 | 100 | 14 | 36 | 36 |
| Petroleum | 100 | 57 | 100 | 100 | 100 | 100 | 14 | 100 | 100 | 29 | 100 | — | — | 29 |
| Primary Metals | 100 | 28 | 76 | 96 | 96 | 100 | 4 | 96 | 76 | 76 | 100 | 52 | — | — |
| Printing | 100 | 50 | 13 | 100 | 100 | 100 | 13 | 100 | 25 | 38 | 100 | 13 | 63 | 13 |
| Rubber | 100 | 17 | 33 | 100 | 100 | 100 | — | 100 | 50 | 50 | 100 | 83 | 50 | 17 |
| Stone, Clay & Glass | 100 | 23 | 62 | 92 | 100 | 100 | 38 | 100 | 77 | 62 | 92 | 8 | 15 | 15 |
| Textiles | 100 | 20 | 30 | 60 | 90 | 100 | — | 100 | 30 | 60 | 100 | 10 | — | 20 |
| Transportation Equipment | 100 | 9 | 59 | 97 | 97 | 100 | 3 | 100 | 100 | 79 | 100 | 88 | 6 | 12 |
| NON-MANUFACTURING | 95 | 41 | 19 | 94 | 96 | 95 | 27 | 97 | 28 | 23 | 97 | 9 | 32 | 13 |
| Communications | 100 | 60 | 20 | 100 | 90 | 90 | 30 | 100 | 50 | 20 | 100 | 10 | 30 | 30 |
| Construction | 100 | 24 | 7 | 100 | 100 | 97 | 24 | 100 | 34 | 3 | 100 | — | — | — |
| Insurance & Finance | 86 | 57 | 29 | 86 | 86 | 86 | 29 | 86 | 57 | 43 | 86 | 29 | — | 29 |
| Maritime | 100 | 100 | 38 | 100 | 100 | 100 | 100 | 100 | — | 38 | 100 | 25 | — | — |
| Mining | 92 | 17 | 42 | 92 | 100 | 100 | 8 | 100 | 58 | 75 | 100 | 17 | 25 | — |
| Retail | 100 | 37 | — | 89 | 100 | 96 | 26 | 100 | 7 | 19 | 100 | 4 | 67 | 4 |
| Services | 93 | 44 | 11 | 93 | 96 | 96 | — | 96 | 4 | 11 | 96 | 11 | 41 | 26 |
| Transportation | 84 | 36 | 24 | 88 | 88 | 88 | 24 | 88 | 28 | 16 | 88 | 4 | 52 | 20 |
| Utilities | 100 | 60 | 60 | 100 | 100 | 100 | 80 | 100 | 70 | 60 | 100 | 20 | 10 | 20 |

## Holiday Pay Provisions

*(Frequency Expressed as Percentage of Contracts)*

|  | Holidays Provided | All Named Holidays Paid | Some Named Holidays Paid |
|---|---|---|---|
| All Industries | 99 | 98 | 1 |
| Manufacturing | 100 | 99 | 1 |
| Non-manufacturing | 97 | 97 | 1 |

# Eligibility for Holiday Pay

Eligibility requirements for holiday pay generally are of two types: a length-of-service requirement and a work requirement. At least one of these two requirements is found in 88 percent of contracts with holiday pay provisions; in many cases both requirements appear. Eligibility requirements are found in 93 percent of manufacturing holiday pay provisions and 77 percent of non-manufacturing provisions.

*Length-of-service requirements* are found in 54 percent of holiday pay provisions. Four weeks is the most common length-of-service requirement, found in 37 percent of clauses specifying such requirements. Three months of service is required under 22 percent of length-of-service requirements, two months under 19 percent, and six weeks under 10 percent. Two length-of-service requirements are for less than four weeks duration, while 19 are for more than three months, up to a maximum of one year of service. The service period required often is equal to the length of the probationary period.

*Work requirements appear* in 84 percent of holiday pay provisions. In nearly four-fifths of work requirement provisions, an employee must work both the day before and the day after a holiday to receive holiday pay. Nine percent call for work at some time during the week, 4 percent require work only on the day before or after a holiday, and 8 percent specify some other requirement, generally more liberal. Under 91 percent of these provisions, work requirements may be waived for excused absences or layoffs.

Additionally, an employee who fails to report for scheduled holiday work is denied holiday pay under 44 percent of holiday pay provisions.

*Industry pattern:* Length-of-service requirements appear in 59 percent of holiday pay provisions in manufacturing industry contracts and 43 percent of those in non-manufacturing. Work requirements are specified in 90 percent of manufacturing holiday pay clauses and 73 percent of those in non-manufacturing. Showing up for scheduled holiday work is a requirement in 53 percent of manufacturing and 22 percent of non-manufacturing holiday pay clauses.

Length-of-service requirements appear in all holiday pay provisions in furniture and leather, and in two-thirds or more of provisions in electrical machinery, lumber, mining, paper, primary metals, stone-clay-glass, textiles, and transportation equipment. Work requirements are found in every holiday pay clause in foods, leather, lumber, paper, rubber, and stone-clay-glass, and in more than four-fifths of provisions in apparel, electrical machinery, furniture, machinery, mining, petroleum, primary metals, retail, textiles, and transportation equipment.

Provisions calling for waiver of work requirements appear in all contracts in leather, lumber, paper, rubber, and stone-clay-glass, and in a majority of agreements in all other industries, except construction, insurance and finance, maritime, transportation, and utilities.

## Holidays Falling on Scheduled Time Off _____

Provision for a holiday occurring on Saturday is found in 39 percent of the total sample. In 82 percent of these clauses an alternate day off is granted, while only pay is provided in 17 percent. Saturday holiday clauses appear in 49 percent of manufacturing contracts and in 25 percent of non-manufacturing contracts.

*Holidays falling on Sunday* are referred to in 66 percent of agreements analyzed—71 percent in manufacturing and 56 percent in non-manufacturing. An alternate day off is arranged in 98 percent of these provisions.

In addition to contracts that specify arrangements for holidays falling on Saturday or Sunday, a number of contracts contain general provisions stating that all holidays will be celebrated regardless of the day on which they fall or that holidays will be celebrated on days observed by the federal or state government. Further, some contracts list specific dates on which holidays are to be observed during the life of the agreement.

Provision for a holiday occurring on an employee's day off is found in 19 percent of the sample, and such clauses are more prevalent in non-manufacturing (28 percent) than in manufacturing (13 percent). An alternate day off is provided under a majority of these provisions, while pay only is provided in 43 percent. In 1 percent, a holiday falling on an employee's day off is forfeited. Provisions for alternate days off prevail in non-manufacturing agreements; clauses stipulating pay only prevail in manufacturing agreements.

*Holidays falling during an employee's vacation* are discussed in 71 percent of contracts studied. Of these provisions, 44 percent provide pay only, 31 percent call for an additional day off, and 25 percent permit either an extra day's pay or an extra day off. Of clauses providing an option, more than one-third leave the choice to employees. Provision for holidays during a vacation are more frequent in manufacturing (78 percent) than in non-manufacturing (61 percent). Pay only is more common in manufacturing, while an alternate day off is more common in non-manufacturing.

## Pay for Holidays Worked _____

Compensation for holiday work is provided in 96 percent of sample contracts. Pay for holiday work is expressed as holiday pay plus pay for hours actually worked in 66 percent of these provisions and as pay only for hours worked in 31 percent. Two percent provide some other type of compensation such as a different rate of pay for work on different holidays. Compensation for holiday work in the form of compensatory time off, appearing in only a small percentage of contracts in early studies, was found in only one contract (retail).

Under contracts discussing compensation for work on a holiday, the most common payments are holiday pay plus doubletime (29 percent), and holiday pay plus time and one-half (28 percent). Following in frequency are pay only for hours worked at doubletime (13 percent), pay only for hours worked at doubletime and one-half (12 percent), and holiday pay plus straight-time (5 percent).

A higher premium after a certain number of hours worked on a holiday is specified in 11 percent of pay for holiday work provisions. In almost all cases the higher premium is applied to hours after a full shift has been worked or to hours outside the normal schedule.

### Rate of Pay for Holiday Work

*(Frequency Expressed as Percentage of Holiday Work Provisions)*

|  | Holiday Pay Plus Pay for Hours Worked at: | | | Pay Only for Hours Worked at: | | | |
|---|---|---|---|---|---|---|---|
|  | 1 | 1½ | 2 | 1½ | 2 | 2½ | 3 |
| All Industries | 5 | 28 | 29 | 2 | 13 | 12 | 4 |
| Manufacturing | 3 | 28 | 39 | 2 | 6 | 11 | 5 |
| Non-manufacturing | 9 | 29 | 11 | 3 | 24 | 12 | 3 |

*Industry pattern:* Premium pay for holiday work is higher in manufacturing agreements than in non-manufacturing agreements. While pay only for hours worked at tripletime occurs in 5 percent of manufacturing and 3 percent of non-manufacturing agreements, holiday pay plus doubletime appears in 39 percent of manufacturing holiday work provisions, compared with 11 percent of non-manufacturing provisions. On the other hand, holiday pay plus straight-time appears in 3 percent of provisions in manufacturing and 9 percent in non-manufacturing, and pay only for hours worked at doubletime is found in 6 percent of provisions in manufacturing and 24 percent in non-manufacturing.

The highest premiums (tripletime for hours worked or holiday pay plus doubletime) predominate in electrical machinery, fabricated metals, furniture, machinery, rubber, and transportation equipment, and are found frequently in primary metals, foods, and retail. The lowest premiums (holiday pay plus straight-time or doubletime for hours worked) predominate in construction and printing, and appear frequently in transportation and services.

## Limitations Upon Management

Restrictions on management's right to schedule work on holidays are found in 27 percent of the sample. Nearly three-quarters of these clauses consist of a limited prohibition on holiday work; more than one-quarter require advance notice. Only four contracts in the sample flatly forbid work on holidays.

*A minimum work or pay guarantee* is applied specifically to holiday work in 20 percent of the sample. In 44 percent of these provisions four hours must be paid or provided. Eight hours is the minimum in 27 percent of the clauses and two hours is the minimum in 13 percent. The guaranteed minimum is to be paid at higher than straight-time in 59 percent of these provisions.

*Industry pattern:* Restrictions on holiday work are more frequent in non-manufacturing (35 percent) than manufacturing (21 percent). Restrictions are most prevalent in agreements in construction (55 percent) and utilities, furniture, and maritime (each 50 percent). They also appear with frequency in lumber (43 percent), retail (41 percent), apparel and rubber (each 33 percent), transporation (32 percent), paper (29 percent), transportation equipment (26 percent), and leather, mining, and printing (each 25 percent).

Minimum work or pay guarantees also are more common in non-manufacturing contracts (28 percent) than manufacturing agreements (14 percent). A minimum guarantee is found in 50 percent each of communications and rubber contracts; one-third to one-half of contracts in maritime, printing, and utilities; and one-quarter to one-third of contracts in construction, insurance and finance, chemicals, foods, mining, petroleum, and transportation.

# 9

## Layoff, Rehiring, and Work Sharing

Layoff provisions are included in 91 percent of the Basic Patterns database. Seniority is a factor in selecting employees for layoff in 87 percent of the contracts—95 percent in manufacturing and 74 percent in non-manufacturing.

Geographic analysis of the sample contracts indicates that layoff provisions are prevalent in all regions designated in the database, ranging from 80 percent in each the Rocky Mountain area and West Coast area to 100 percent in the Midwest.

*Seniority is the sole consideration* in selecting employees to be laid off in 46 percent of sample contracts.

*Seniority is the determining factor* in layoffs under 28 percent of the contracts included in the study. These provisions call for retention of more senior employees during a reduction in force only if they are qualified for available jobs.

*Seniority is a secondary factor,* to be considered only when factors such as ability and physical fitness are equal, in 12 percent of the contracts.

*Industry pattern:* Seniority is the sole or determining factor in at least two-thirds each of manufacturing industry contracts and non-manufacturing industry contracts except those in construction and maritime.

### Consideration of Seniority in Layoff

*(Frequency Expressed as Percentage of Contracts)*

|  | Applied in Some Degree | Sole Factor | Determining Factor | Secondary Factor |
|---|---|---|---|---|
| All Industries | 87 | 46 | 28 | 12 |
| Manufacturing | 95 | 47 | 34 | 13 |
| Non-manufacturing | 74 | 44 | 19 | 10 |

## Exceptions from Seniority Rules in Layoffs

Exceptions from seniority in layoffs are allowed in 47 percent of the sample contracts, and more than three-fourths of these provisions give union representatives superseniority for layoff purposes. Under superseniority provisions, union stewards and local officials are the last employees to be laid off. Of contracts granting union representatives superseniority, 38 percent stipulate that the representatives must be qualified for available jobs to be exempt from layoff provisions.

*Industry pattern:* Union representatives are given top seniority for layoff purposes in at least half the contracts in the following industries: textiles, electrical machinery, fabricated metals, furniture, machinery, primary metals, and transportation equipment.

Specially skilled employees, whose employment is necessary for continuous and efficient company operations, are exempt from layoff provisions in 23 percent of procedures containing seniority exceptions.

Seniority rules may be waived during temporary (usually less than two weeks) or emergency layoffs in 38 percent of contracts specifying exceptions to layoff procedures—40 percent in manufacturing and 30 percent in non-manufacturing.

Seniority employees may elect layoff out of order in 12 percent of sample contracts—17 percent in manufacturing and 5 percent in non-manufacturing.

## Notice of Layoff

Advance notice of layoff is required in 49 percent of sample agreements—57 percent of manufacturing contracts and 37 percent of non-manufacturing contracts. Most (96 percent) of the layoff notice clauses require the company to give notice of impending layoff to the affected employee, the union, or both.

Of contracts requiring advance notice of layoffs, 38 percent specify notification to the employee; 22 percent specify notification to the union; 36 percent specify notification to both.

### Advance Notice to Employees

*(Frequency Expressed as Percentage of Notice Provisions)*

|  | No Minimum | 1 or 2 Days | 3 or 4 Days | 5 Days | 7 or More Days |
|---|---|---|---|---|---|
| All Industries | 6 | 16 | 15 | 19 | 13 |
| Manufacturing | 6 | 22 | 18 | 18 | 4 |
| Non-manufacturing | 5 | — | 9 | 21 | 35 |

### Advance Notice to Unions

*(Frequency Expressed as Percentage of Notice Provisions)*

|  | No Minimum | 1 or 2 Days | 3 or 4 Days | 5 Days | 7 or More Days |
|---|---|---|---|---|---|
| All Industries | 12 | 12 | 11 | 11 | 10 |
| Manufacturing | 12 | 16 | 14 | 11 | 6 |
| Non-manufacturing | 11 | 2 | 4 | 9 | 18 |

Under agreements specifying amount of advance layoff notice to employees, 49 percent stipulate one to four days' notice; 51 percent stipulate five days or more. In contracts specifying amount of notice to the union, 53 percent require one to four days' notice; 47 percent require five or more days.

*Industry pattern:* Notice-of-layoff provisions are found in at least two-thirds of contracts in communications, electrical machinery, fabricated metals, furniture, machinery, printing, rubber, and transportation equipment industries.

# Bumping

Employees scheduled for layoff are permitted to displace less senior employees in other jobs under 59 percent of agreements included in the survey—72 percent in manufacturing and 39 percent in non-manufacturing.

Of bumping rights clauses, 65 percent state that employees must be qualified to perform the job they desire to bump into. Service requirements ranging from one to 16 years are required in 7 percent of bumping provisions, and break-in periods for employees to demonstrate their qualifications for the job are called for in 21 percent.

*Bumping throughout the company* is permitted in 5 percent of contracts specifying the permissible bumping area; bumping throughout the plant in 22 percent. Bumping is restricted to a division or department in 17 percent of these clauses, while in 52 percent bumping is restricted to an employee's classification or group. Four percent, of the provisions allow employees to bump only to their former job, classification, or group.

Of the 92 percent of bumping provisions specifying who may be displaced, 64 percent specify the least senior employee, and 35 percent specify any less senior employee.

*Industry pattern:* Bumping is allowed in at least three-quarters of contracts in the following industries: chemicals, electrical machinery, leather, machinery, furniture, mining, primary metals, rubber, and textiles. At least 60 percent of electrical machinery, furniture, leather, machinery, paper, primary metals, rubber, and textiles industry agreements specify that an employee desiring to exercise bumping rights must be qualified to perform the job.

# Recall

Recall of employees after layoff is provided for in 81 percent of contracts in the database. Of these provisions, 41 percent recall employees in reverse order of layoff, and 49 percent recall employees in reverse order of layoff only if they are qualified to perform available jobs. Laid-off employees have preference over new hires in 36 percent of contracts containing recall provisions.

# Work Sharing

Clauses providing for work sharing as an alternative or prelude to layoffs are included in 18 percent of the sample—24 percent in manufacturing and 7 percent in non-manufacturing. Of contracts providing for work sharing, 44 percent specify that work sharing will be implemented for a limited time, and 34 percent state that the company must consult with the union before work sharing may be implemented.

## Layoff Provisions

*(Frequency Expressed as Percentage of Industry Contracts)*

| | Seniority Applied in Layoffs | Exceptions From Seniority allowed | Advance Notice of Layoff Required | Recall After Layoff Specified | Bumping Permitted | Worksharing Provided |
|---|---|---|---|---|---|---|
| ALL INDUS- TRIES | 87 | 47 | 49 | 81 | 59 | 18 |
| MANUFACTUR- ING | 95 | 64 | 57 | 90 | 72 | 24 |
| Apparel | 78 | 11 | — | 78 | — | 89 |
| Chemicals | 100 | 75 | 56 | 81 | 75 | 6 |
| Electrical Machinery | 95 | 90 | 75 | 95 | 90 | 25 |
| Fabricated Metals | 95 | 74 | 74 | 89 | 74 | 32 |
| Foods | 100 | 33 | 57 | 95 | 62 | — |
| Furniture | 100 | 100 | 67 | 100 | 83 | 33 |
| Leather | 100 | 25 | 25 | 75 | 100 | 50 |
| Lumber | 100 | 43 | 29 | 100 | 57 | — |
| Machinery | 100 | 92 | 77 | 96 | 88 | 46 |
| Paper | 86 | 43 | 43 | 79 | 64 | 7 |
| Petroleum | 100 | — | 57 | 86 | 57 | — |
| Primary Metals | 96 | 76 | 48 | 96 | 92 | 20 |
| Printing | 88 | — | 75 | 50 | 38 | — |
| Rubber | 83 | 17 | 83 | 100 | 83 | 33 |
| Stone-Clay-Glass | 92 | 31 | 31 | 92 | 62 | 38 |
| Textiles | 100 | 90 | 20 | 90 | 90 | 20 |
| Transportation Equipment | 91 | 94 | 71 | 94 | 68 | 24 |
| NON-MANU- FACTURING | 74 | 19 | 37 | 67 | 39 | 7 |
| Communications | 100 | 20 | 100 | 100 | 70 | 30 |
| Construction | 10 | 10 | 14 | 7 | — | 3 |
| Insurance & Finance | 71 | 29 | 29 | 71 | 57 | — |
| Maritime | 38 | — | — | 38 | — | — |
| Mining | 83 | 50 | 33 | 92 | 75 | 8 |
| Retail | 96 | 33 | 33 | 93 | 37 | 11 |
| Services | 96 | 11 | 37 | 81 | 41 | 7 |
| Transportation | 92 | 20 | 60 | 72 | 64 | — |
| Utilities | 90 | — | 30 | 70 | 30 | 10 |

# 10

# Leave of Absence

Leave of absence provisions appear in 92 percent of the 400 sample contracts contained in CBNC's database, the same percentage as in the 1986 Basic Patterns study. Geographic analysis shows that from 70 to 96 percent of contracts in regions designated in the database contain leave provisions.

Some form of leave of absence is provided for in all but one manufacturing agreement and in all but three non-manufacturing contracts outside the construction industry; only one construction contract includes a leave of absence provision. Eight major types of leave are included in the study—personal, union business, military, family, civic duty, funeral, unpaid sick leave, and paid sick leave.

### Leave of Absence Provisions

*(Frequency Expressed as Percentage of Contracts)*

|  | Per-sonal | Union | Fam-ily | Fu-neral | Civic | Paid Sick | Unpaid Sick | Mili-tary |
|---|---|---|---|---|---|---|---|---|
| All Industries | 76 | 77 | 34 | 85 | 81 | 31 | 53 | 74 |
| Manufacturing | 84 | 87 | 36 | 95 | 93 | 20 | 57 | 84 |
| Non-manufacturing | 63 | 61 | 32 | 68 | 63 | 47 | 47 | 59 |

## Personal Leave

Leave of absence for personal or unspecified reasons is provided in 76 percent of agreements contained in the database. Some contracts simply state that personal leave will be granted for "good" or "sufficient" reason, subject to the approval of the employer, while others specify reasons such as family illness or personal business.

*Duration of leave* is mentioned in 77 percent of the contracts allowing personal leave and ranges from one week to five years. Of agreements that discuss duration, 32 percent allow an initial one-month leave period, 21 percent allow three months, and 14 percent specify a "reasonable" or unspecified period. Extension of the initial leave period is allowed in 46 percent of personal leave provisions analyzed.

*Effect on seniority* is discussed in 70 percent of personal leave provisions. Of the seniority clauses, 40 percent provide for retention during leave, 55 percent provide for accumulation for the length of leave, and 5 percent provide for accumulation for a specified period and then retention. A time limit is imposed on retention and/or accumulation in 19 percent of the clauses that discuss seniority. It should be noted, however, that contract language on seniority often is ambiguous. *

---

* For purposes of tabulation, clauses stating that "there shall be no loss of seniority during leave" have been considered as providing for retention—without accumulation—of seniority. This method has been followed throughout this section.

*Early return from personal leave* is specifically allowed in 8 percent of personal leave clauses; advance notice of an employee's intent to return to work is required in 7 percent.

*Reemployment rights* are discussed in 33 percent of personal leave clauses. Of agreements containing reemployment rights provisions, 37 percent guarantee employees their former job or an equivalent, 27 percent guarantee the former job or an equivalent if it is not held by a more senior employee, and 24 percent provide a "general right" to reemployment.

*Violation of leave conditions* is discussed in 79 percent of personal leave clauses. Failure to return on time is the most frequently mentioned leave violation, cited in 39 percent of clauses dealing with the subject; failure to return on time except in an emergency or with company approval is cited in 31 percent. Thirty-three percent of violation clauses refer to working elsewhere; 30 percent cite working elsewhere without company approval. Fourteen percent of these clauses cite falsifying an application for leave as a violation. Many contracts specify more than one type of leave violation.

Discharge is a penalty for leave violations in 59 percent of contracts discussing violations; 61 percent impose loss of seniority as a penalty. Both penalties are included in some agreements.

*Approval of personal leave* is a management prerogative in 57 percent of contracts containing personal leave provisions, while both management and union approval is required in 13 percent. Twenty-four percent of personal leave clauses call for management approval with notice to the union.

*Industry pattern:* Personal leave provisions appear in 84 percent of manufacturing contracts and 63 percent (or 78 percent excluding construction) of non-manufacturing agreements. Personal leave is provided for in all furniture, rubber, and leather industry contracts, and in all but one each of communications, lumber, fabricated metals, petroleum, and apparel agreements. Printing, insurance and finance, and construction are the only industries in which less than one-half of contracts call for personal leave.

## Union Leave

Leave to perform union duties is found in 77 percent of the contracts in the database—87 percent in manufacturing and 61 percent in non-manufacturing.

*Long-term leave* to assume union office or to participate in other union business is provided in 70 percent of the contracts analyzed. These provisions are found in 81 percent of manufacturing agreements and in 52 percent of non-manufacturing contracts. More than one-third (37 percent) of long-term leave provisions limit the number of employees who may be granted such leave at the same time.

*Duration* of long-term leave is specified in 88 percent of contracts providing such leave. Of clauses specifying duration, leave for a one-year period is specified in 36 percent; for term of office in 34 percent. In 8 percent of these provisions leave for a two-year period is allowed. Extension of the initial leave period is allowed in 43 percent of long-term leave provisions.

*Effect on seniority* is discussed in 90 percent of long-term union leave provisions. Seniority accumulates for the length of leave in 65 percent of the seniority provisions and is retained in 33 percent. Only 2 percent of these clauses provide for accumulation for a specified period followed by retention.

*Short-term leave* to attend union conventions and conferences is allowed in 47 percent of contracts in the database and is more common in manufacturing agreements (50 percent) than in non-manufacturing agreements (41 percent). The number of employees permitted to take short-term leave at one time is restricted in 48 percent of such clauses.

*Industry pattern:* All contracts in rubber, textiles, fabricated metals, communications, insurance and finance, furniture, and leather industries provide for union leave. These provisions are included in three-quarters or more of contracts in 11 other industries. Only in printing, services, apparel, and construction industries do less than one-half of agreements contain union leave provisions.

### Union Leave Provisions

*(Frequency Expressed as Number of Contracts)*

| | | Long-Term Leave | | | | | | Short-Term Leave | |
| | | Length of Leave Permitted | | | | | No. of employ-ees on leave limited | No. of employ-ees on leave limited | |
| | No. of provi-sions | Term of Office | Term of Contract | Less than one year | One year | More than one year | | No. of provi-sions | No. of employ-ees on leave limited |
|---|---|---|---|---|---|---|---|---|---|
| All Industries | 307 | 84 | 8 | 13 | 88 | 52 | 103 | 186 | 90 |
| Manufacturing | 213 | 56 | 5 | 9 | 71 | 37 | 88 | 122 | 64 |
| Non-manufacturing | 94 | 28 | 3 | 4 | 17 | 15 | 15 | 64 | 26 |

## Family Leave

Family leave provisions are found in 34 percent of sample agreements. All of the contracts provide for maternity leave, and 9 percent include paternity leave, child-care leave, and/or leave in conjunction with adopting a child.

*Eligibility for maternity leave* is based on length of service under 21 percent of maternity leave clauses. Three months of service is the most common requirement, appearing in nine of the 28 contracts containing service requirements. Seven contracts require two months of service and six require one year of service. Twenty-three percent of maternity leave provisions require a physical examination or medical certificate upon return from leave.

**Duration** is discussed in 79 percent of maternity leave provisions and varies from two months to three years. Under agreements specifying leave duration, the most common periods allowed are six months (19 percent), and one year (18 percent). Leave for four months is granted in 5 percent of such clauses, and 2 percent each permit leave for two months, three months, and 15 months. Length of maternity leave is determined by a physician in 22 percent of the contracts that discuss duration.

**Effect on seniority** is discussed in 75 percent of maternity leave provisions. Of these, 58 percent allow accumulation of seniority; 37 percent allow retention of seniority. Seniority is accumulated for a specified period of time and then retained in 5 percent of these clauses.

*Industry pattern:* Maternity leave is provided in 36 percent of manufacturing agreements and 32 percent of non-manufacturing contracts. Such leave is provided in one-half or more of contracts in furniture, rubber, transportation equipment, leather, textiles, electrical machinery, apparel, transportation, and service industries.

### Service Requirement For Maternity Leave

*(Frequency Expressed as Number of Contracts)*

|  | Number of Months | | | | | |
| --- | --- | --- | --- | --- | --- | --- |
|  | 1 | 2 | 3 | 4 | 6 | 12 |
| All Industries | 2 | 7 | 9 | 1 | 3 | 6 |
| Manufacturing | 1 | 6 | 6 | 1 | 1 | 1 |
| Non-manufacturing | 1 | 1 | 3 | 0 | 2 | 5 |

### Length of Maternity Leave

*(Frequency Expressed as Number of Contracts)*

|  | "Reasonable time" | Set by physician | Maximum Number of Months | | | | | | | |
| --- | --- | --- | --- | --- | --- | --- | --- | --- | --- | --- |
|  |  |  | 2 | 3 | 4 | 6 | 9 | 12 | 18 | 36 |
| All Industries | 3 | 24 | 2 | 2 | 5 | 20 | 3 | 19 | 1 | 1 |
| Manufacturing | 2 | 20 | 1 | 2 | 3 | 11 | 1 | 13 | 1 | 1 |
| Non-manufacturing | 1 | 4 | 1 | 0 | 2 | 9 | 2 | 6 | 0 | 0 |

## Funeral Leave

Time off for death in an employee's immediate family (as defined by the contract) is granted under 85 percent of sample contracts in the database.

*Three days' leave* is granted in 85 percent of bereavement clauses, followed by five days' leave in 5 percent, and four days' leave in 4 percent of clauses. Thirty-two percent of bereavement clauses grant shorter leaves for death outside the immediate family (as defined by the contract). Of bereavement leave provisions, 40 percent require an employee to attend the funeral, while 22 percent specify that proof of death may be required upon return from funeral leave. Only four of the sample contracts charge time spent on bereavement leave against sick or annual leave.

*Industry pattern:* Funeral leave is more common in manufacturing agreements (95 percent) than in non-manufacturing (68 percent). All contracts in the chemical, communications, mining, furniture, paper, rubber, leather, petroleum, electrical machinery, lumber, and fabricated metals industries provide funeral leave. Insurance and finance, maritime, and construction are the only industries in which less than one-half of the contracts provide funeral leave.

## Civic Duty Leave

Leave to perform civic duty appears in 81 percent of agreements in the database. All but one of these contracts specify leave for jury duty, and 29 percent grant leave for other court service.

Payment of an employee's regular salary less any jury fees received is provided in 83 percent of jury duty clauses, and payment of full salary regardless of jury fees received is provided in 15 percent. Employees are paid a specified flat amount in 1 percent of jury duty provisions, and another 1 percent are silent on the subject of compensation. Twenty-nine percent of jury duty provisions require an employee to work when possible, while 16 percent limit the number of days per year an employee may be paid by the company for jury service.

*Leave to assume public office* is found in 17 percent of the 400 sample contracts. Duration of such leave is usually limited to one term of office. Six percent of agreements studied allow leave for service in the Peace Corps, and 2 percent allow leave to work in a credit union.

*Effect on seniority* is discussed in 71 percent of civic duty provisions (other than jury duty or other court service). Of these, 70 percent allow accumulation of seniority and 24 percent provide for retention.

*Industry pattern:* Civic duty leave appears in 93 percent of manufacturing contracts and in 63 percent of non-manufacturing. At least three-fourths of contracts in foods, furniture, lumber, mining, primary metals, printing, retail, machinery, stone-clay-glass, transportation, and transportation equipment provide civic duty leave. All contracts in textiles, paper, chemicals, fabricated metals, leather, petroleum, rubber, electrical machinery, and communications provide civic duty leave.

## Paid Sick Leave _____

Paid sick leave, not sickness and accident insurance (*see section 44*), is provided in 31 percent of the sample contracts.

A length-of-service requirement appears in 67 percent of paid sick leave provisions. One year of service is required in 31 percent of paid leave clauses; six months in 16 percent; and less than six months in another 16 percent. A service requirement of more than one year is found in 4 percent of paid sick leave provisions.

*Duration* is specified in 97 percent of paid sick leave clauses. Thirty-eight percent of sick leave clauses grant leave for a flat period of time. Leave is earned on the basis of a specified number of credits per unit of worktime in 32 percent of sick leave provisions. Under 25 percent of sick leave clauses, duration varies with an employee's length of service.

Restrictions are placed on accumulation of unused sick leave in 51 percent of paid sick leave provisions. Employees are paid for unused leave in 46 percent of contracts providing paid sick leave, usually at annual intervals.

Amount of pay granted during sick leave is specified in 89 percent of paid sick leave clauses. Of these, 88 percent provide full pay for the entire period; 7 percent provide partial pay for the entire period; five percent provide full pay for a specified period followed by partial pay for the remaining leave time.

*Waiting periods,* ranging from one day to 10 days of absence before sick leave pay takes effect, are found in 29 percent of paid sick leave provisions. The most common period is one day, found in 46 percent of waiting period clauses, followed by two days in 29 percent.

*Industry pattern:* Paid sick leave provisions appear in more non-manufacturing agreements, 47 percent, than in manufacturing agreements, 20 percent. They are found in one-half or more of contracts in seven industries—utilities (80 percent), transportation (76 percent), communications (60 percent), retail and services (each 59 percent), insurance and finance (57 percent), and printing (50 percent). These provisions are absent from apparel, lumber, rubber, leather, primary metals, maritime, and construction industry contracts.

## Unpaid Sick Leave _____

Unpaid sick leave is provided in 53 percent of the contracts contained in the database. A length-of-service requirement must be met in 13 percent of these clauses. Of agreements containing length-of-service requirements, 25 percent specify one year of service, and 75 percent specify six months or less.

*Duration* of leave is discussed in 74 percent of unpaid sick leave clauses. Of these, 64 percent set a flat length of time ranging from one month to five years. One month, three months, six months, and one year are the most common periods of leave granted. Eight percent of unpaid sick leave provisions grant leave for the duration of an illness or until a doctor approves a return from leave. Length of leave is determined by an employee's length of service in 10 percent of clauses discussing duration.

Of unpaid sick leave provisions, 37 percent allow extension of the initial leave; 61 percent specify that a medical certification of illness or injury may be required.

***Effect on seniority*** is discussed in 74 percent of unpaid sick leave provisions. Seniority accumulates for the full leave period under 60 percent of clauses mentioning the subject; seniority accumulates for a time and then is retained under 6 percent; seniority is retained for the entire period under 34 percent. Thirty-nine percent of seniority provisions place a limit on retention or accumulation.

*Industry pattern:* Unpaid sick leave provisions appear in 57 percent of anufacturing contracts and 47 percent of non-manufacturing agreements. Such leave is provided in all leather contracts and in two-thirds or more of sample contracts in transportation equipment (88 percent), transportation (80 percent), services (70 percent), and rubber (67 percent). Unpaid sick leave is found in at least one-half of contracts in 11 other industries.

## Military Leave

Long-term military leave is mentioned in 70 percent of the sample. A special bonus is paid upon entering military service in 9 percent of these clauses. Special provisions for returning disabled veterans are found in 14 percent of long-term military leave clauses; educational leave for veterans in 8 percent.

***Short-term military leave*** for reserve training is mentioned in 38 percent of contracts analyzed. Pay while on short-term leave is discussed in 84 percent of these clauses. Of pay provisions, 91 percent guarantee the difference between regular pay and military pay. Length of leave is discussed in 84 percent of short-term leave provisions, with two weeks specified most frequently (70 percent).

*Industry pattern:* Military leave provisions appear in 84 percent of manufacturing agreements, 59 percent of non-manufacturing contracts, and in at least one-half of contracts in all industries except construction.

## Leave of Absence Provisions

*(Frequency Expressed as Percentage of Contracts in each Region)*

| | All Types | Person-al | Union | Family | Funeral | Civic | Paid Sick | Unpaid Sick | Mili-tary |
|---|---|---|---|---|---|---|---|---|---|
| | | | | | Type of Leave | | | | |
| All Regions | 92 | 76 | 77 | 34 | 85 | 81 | 31 | 53 | 74 |
| Middle Atlantic | 93 | 74 | 76 | 36 | 88 | 80 | 39 | 51 | 78 |
| Midwest | 96 | 63 | 75 | 21 | 88 | 83 | 33 | 54 | 83 |
| New England | 88 | 80 | 72 | 44 | 84 | 76 | 40 | 52 | 80 |
| North Central | 96 | 84 | 87 | 37 | 93 | 89 | 11 | 63 | 78 |
| Rocky Mountain | 70 | 50 | 50 | 20 | 50 | 60 | 30 | 50 | 40 |
| Southeast | 96 | 68 | 84 | 24 | 86 | 88 | 22 | 38 | 74 |
| Southwest | 77 | 77 | 54 | 15 | 69 | 77 | 8 | 46 | 62 |
| West Coast | 85 | 78 | 50 | 33 | 72 | 70 | 52 | 46 | 48 |
| Multiregion | 95 | 80 | 90 | 43 | 83 | 80 | 38 | 60 | 87 |

# 11

# Management and Union Rights

Management and union rights provisions are found in all the 400 sample contracts included in the Basic Patterns database.

Management rights generally are stated in a contract section labeled as such, while union rights usually are scattered throughout a contract according to subject matter.

Management rights statements are found in 79 percent of agreements analyzed. Of these, 76 percent reserve to management direction of the working force, 72 percent management of the company business, and 37 percent each control of production methods and right to frame company rules.

Other designated prerogatives found in management clauses are: determining employees' duties, 27 percent; closing or relocating a plant, 16 percent; instituting technological changes, 14 percent. 10 percent.

*Industry pattern:* Management rights statements appear in 83 percent of manufacturing contracts and 71 percent of non-manufacturing agreements. They are found in all textiles, mining, insurance and finance, lumber, rubber, leather, and furniture contracts, and in at least 90 percent of chemicals, primary metals, transportation equipment, utilities, and services agreements. In fabricated metals, electrical machinery, machinery, and paper management rights are listed in from 85 to 89 percent of agreements studied. Further, management rights statements appear in 50 percent or more of contracts in the remaining industries with the exception of apparel, construction, and printing.

## Management Rights Provisions

*(Frequency Expressed as Percentage of Management Rights Statements)*

|  | All Industries | Manufacturing | Non-manufacturing |
|---|---|---|---|
| Direct Work Force | 76 | 77 | 75 |
| Manage Business | 72 | 73 | 70 |
| Control Production | 37 | 48 | 18 |
| Frame Company Rules | 37 | 36 | 39 |
| Determine Employees' Duties | 27 | 24 | 33 |
| Close or Relocate Plant | 16 | 17 | 14 |
| Change Technology | 14 | 17 | 9 |

**Savings clauses** appear in 44 percent of agreements, the same frequency as recorded in the 1986 study. They appear in 47 percent of manufacturing and 39 percent of non-manufacturing agreements. Of savings provisions, 63 percent state that management retains all rights not specifically modified or restricted by the contract; 60 percent state that management rights listed in the agreement are not necessarily all inclusive.

## Restriction on Management Rights _____

Restrictions are placed on management in 86 percent of sample contracts—90 percent in manufacturing and 79 percent in non-manufacturing. Slightly more than one-half (53 percent) of agreements surveyed contain a general statement restricting management prerogatives. Of these, 95 percent prohibit management from taking actions in violation of the contract terms, and 17 percent specify that management actions are subject to the grievance and/or arbitration procedure.

*Industry pattern:* Some restriction is placed on management rights in all utilities, maritime, petroleum, rubber, apparel, electrical machinery, mining, and insurance and finance contracts. Such provisions are found in 90 percent or more of communications, fabricated metals, transportation equipment, primary metals, paper, and chemicals agreements. At least 80 percent of contracts in all other industries except leather (75 percent), transportation (64 percent), printing (63 percent), lumber (57 percent), and retail (56 percent), contain some form of restriction on management rights.

***Subcontracting*** is mentioned in 54 percent of the sample contracts—51 percent in manufacturing and 59 percent in non-manufacturing. In 48 percent (up from 45 percent in the 1986 study and 36 percent in 1983) of the subcontracting clauses, advance discussion with, or notification to, the union is required; in 26 percent subcontracting is prohibited if layoffs exist or would result from such action. Thirty-six percent of these provisions allow contracting out only if the necessary skills and equipment are not available; 22 percent only if contractual standards are met. Under 18 percent of subcontracting clauses, contracting out must be in accordance with past practice.

*Industry pattern:* Limitations on contracting out are found in 90 percent of construction, 89 percent of apparel, 86 percent of petroleum, 83 percent each of mining and rubber, 80 percent of communications, and 70 percent of utilities agreements. At least 50 percent of furniture, paper, primary metals, machinery, fabricated metals, maritime, and transportation equipment contracts contain subcontracting provisions.

***Supervisory performance*** of bargaining unit work is limited in 56 percent of the sample contracts. Most of these clauses, however, provide that work may be performed by supervisory employees on a limited basis under one or more of the following conditions: for instruction purposes (77 percent), in case of emergency (74 percent), to conduct experiments (28 percent), to develop new products (15 percent), and for demonstration purposes (13 percent). Twenty-four percent of the clauses limiting work by supervisors allow them to work if a regular employee is not displaced, and 20 percent specify for a limited time only. Work by non-union employees—for example, management trainees—is permitted in 12 percent of contracts contained in the sample database.

*Industry pattern:* Work by supervisors is limited in 71 percent of manufacturing agreements and 32 percent of non-manufacturing contracts. From 82 to 92 percent of furniture, mining, rubber, petroleum, machinery, paper, primary metals, and transportation equipment agreements limit work by supervisors. Such limitations also are found in from 50 to 79 percent of lumber, chemicals, communications, utilities, electrical machinery, fabricated metals, foods, textiles, leather, and stone-clay-glass contracts.

## Restrictions on Management Rights

*(Frequency Expressed as Percentage of Contracts)*

|  | All Industries | Manufacturing | Non-manufacturing |
| --- | --- | --- | --- |
| General Statement | 53 | 58 | 46 |
| Subcontracting | 54 | 51 | 59 |
| Supervisory Performance of Work | 56 | 71 | 32 |
| Technological Changes | 27 | 27 | 27 |
| Plant Shutdown or Relocation | 25 | 33 | 13 |

***Technological changes*** are restricted in 27 percent of all contracts analyzed, and in 27 percent each of manufacutring and non-manufacturing agreements. Of these provisions, 63 percent require advance discussion with, or notification to, the union and 12 percent state that the company will make an effort to retain displaced employees. In 25 percent of agreements limiting management's right to institute technological changes, retraining is required, and in 8 percent retraining is required only if an employee qualifies for the newly created job.

*Industry pattern:* Limitations on management's right to make technological changes are specified in 90 percent of communications, 88 percent of printing, 78 percent of apparel, 63 percent of maritime, 50 percent each of textiles and leather contracts, and in from 43 to 33 percent of rubber, petroleum, mining, retail, and insurance and finance agreements.

***Plant shutdown or relocation*** limitations are discussed in 25 percent of agreements analyzed. Advance notice to, or discussion with, the union is required under 68 percent of agreements dealing with the subject. In 44 percent of plant closure clauses, a displaced employee has transfer rights to a new location and in 24 percent the company is required to pay at least a portion of moving costs. Job placement and training programs are called for in 25 percent (up from 17 percent in the 1986 study) of shutdown provisions, while some other form of job security is found in 35 percent of the clauses.

*Industry pattern:* Shutdown and relocation provisions are found in 33 percent of manufacturing contracts and in 13 percent of non-manufacturing agreements. Such clauses appear in 78 percent of apparel, 60 percent of electrical machinery, 57 percent of petroleum, 50 percent each of leather and rubber agreements, and in at least 40 percent of fabricated metals and primary metals contracts. Further, these clauses appear in at least one-quarter of machinery, foods, retail, and transportation equipment industry contracts.

## Union Rights

Provisions stating union rights (use of bulletin boards, number of in-plant representatives, access to information, etc.) are found in 96 percent of contracts in the database—96 percent in manufacturing and 97 percent in non-manufacturing industry agreements.

*Industry pattern:* Union rights provisions appear in from 90 to 100 percent of all industry agreements except fabricated metals (89 percent), maritime and transportation (each 88 percent), lumber (86 percent), printing (75 percent), and petroleum (71 percent).

**In-plant union representatives** are discussed in 55 percent of agreements studied—56 percent in manufacturing and 52 percent in non-manufacturing. Of these contracts, 21 percent specify how many stewards or committeemen are to represent a given number of employees in the bargaining unit, with varying limitations on the maximum number of representatives.

**Access to plant by union representatives** who are not company employees is permitted in 55 percent of agreements in the database—48 percent of manufacturing contracts and 65 percent of non-manufacturing agreements discuss the matter. A majority (70 percent) of access clauses either prohibit union representatives from interfering with production and/or require notification to management of their visit.

**Union access to bulletin boards** is specified in 69 percent of sample agreements—78 percent in manufacturing contracts and 53 percent in non-manufacturing contracts. In 65 percent of these provisions, the company furnishes the bulletin board, in 19 percent the union shares space with the company, in 5 percent the union furnishes its own, and in the remaining 11 percent it is unclear who furnishes the board.

*Industry pattern:* Bulletin board provisions are found in all mining, rubber textiles, and insurance and finance agreements, and in from 80 to 94 percent of furniture, chemicals petroleum, communications, utilities, lumber, electrical machinery, fabricated metals, machinery, paper, transportation equipment, and stone-clay-glass contracts. At least one-half of agreements in foods, leather, primary metals, retail, services, and transportation industries contain bulletin board clauses.

**Restrictions on the use of bulletin boards** are listed in 93 percent of agreements containing bulletin board provisions. The most common restrictions found in these clauses are use only for union business (82 percent), management approval of all postings (46 percent), and management approval of other than routine postings (14 percent). In from 7 to 15 percent of contracts restricting union use of bulletin boards, the union is prohibited from posting anything political, controversial, or derogatory to the company.

*Union's right to information* (other than data such as seniority lists) is stated in 61 percent of the sample—52 percent in manufacturing and 76 in non-manufacturing contracts. Of these provisions, 63 percent require that the union be notified of newly hired employees or of the need for additional employees, 26 percent specify that the union be given access to information on wages, and 15 percent permit union access to personnel data. Sixty-seven percent of these clauses guarantee unions the right to various other information.

*Union labels* or store cards or decals are called for in 10 percent of the sample contracts. Such provisions are found in 78 percent of apparel contracts and in 52 percent of retail agreements.

## Union Rights and Selections

*(Frequency Expressed as Percentage of Contracts)*

|  | All Industries | Manufacturing | Non-manufacturing |
|---|---|---|---|
| Access by Union Representatives | 55 | 48 | 65 |
| Bulletin Board Rights | 69 | 78 | 53 |
| Access to Information | 61 | 52 | 76 |
| **Union Activity on Company Time** | | | |
| No Union Activity | 23 | 29 | 13 |
| No Solicitation of membership | 16 | 21 | 7 |
| No Dues Collection | 9 | 12 | 3 |
| No Distribution of Literature | 7 | 8 | 5 |

## Restricted Rights

Union activity on company time is specifically limited in 35 percent of agreements analyzed—44 percent in manufacturing and 21 percent in non-manufacturing. Of these agreements, 66 percent include a blanket prohibition of "union activity," 45 percent prohibit solicitation of union members, 25 percent prohibit dues collection, and 19 percent prohibit distribution of union literature on company time. Other forms of union activity are forbidden in 7 percent of agreements dealing with the subject.

*Union business procedures* are mentioned in 13 percent of contracts contained in the database, most notably in the construction industry (83 percent). Of these provisions, 57 percent include settlement procedures in instances of jurisdictional disputes and 53 percent ban strikes during jurisdictional disputes.

## Management and Union Rights Provisions

*(Frequency Expressed as Percentage of Contracts in Each Region)*

| | Middle Atlantic | Midwest | New England | North Central | Rocky Mountain | Southeast | Southwest | West Coast | Multiregion |
|---|---|---|---|---|---|---|---|---|---|
| **Management Rights** | 74 | 88 | 76 | 90 | 80 | 90 | 69 | 65 | 68 |
| To Direct Working Force | 49 | 67 | 60 | 69 | 80 | 78 | 54 | 46 | 50 |
| To Manage Company Business | 47 | 63 | 60 | 67 | 70 | 72 | 38 | 35 | 55 |
| To Frame Company Rules | 34 | 21 | 12 | 39 | 20 | 34 | 23 | 20 | 25 |
| **Restrictions on Management Rights** | 86 | 92 | 88 | 93 | 70 | 74 | 85 | 78 | 92 |
| To Subcontract | 59 | 42 | 48 | 48 | 70 | 46 | 62 | 48 | 70 |
| To Close or Relocate Plant | 19 | 21 | 16 | 32 | 10 | 6 | 23 | 13 | 57 |
| To Implement New Technology | 30 | 25 | 24 | 17 | — | 22 | 23 | 30 | 45 |
| **Union Rights** | 95 | 100 | 100 | 94 | 90 | 90 | 92 | 100 | 98 |
| To Bulletin Boards | 61 | 75 | 64 | 78 | 40 | 78 | 69 | 54 | 72 |
| To Information | 64 | 58 | 64 | 49 | 60 | 50 | 54 | 76 | 75 |
| To Plant Entry By Union Officers | 51 | 42 | 68 | 36 | 60 | 52 | 62 | 96 | 55 |
| **Restrictions on Union Rights** (on company time) | 39 | 38 | 20 | 37 | 20 | 50 | 31 | 11 | 40 |
| Ban on Any Union Activity | 27 | 56 | 8 | 28 | 20 | 34 | 15 | 9 | 22 |
| Ban on Dues Collection | 10 | 22 | — | 8 | — | 14 | 15 | 2 | 12 |
| Ban on Solicitation of Membership | 17 | 67 | 12 | 15 | — | 22 | 23 | 2 | 18 |

## Union-Management Cooperation

Union-management cooperation pledges are found in 53 percent of contracts studied—up from 45 percent in the 1986 study, 37 percent in the 1983, study, and 25 percent in the 1979 study. Of these provisions, 28 percent call for formation of joint committees to explore specific problems, such as absenteeism or productivity. Fifteen percent of the clauses stipulate establishment of joint committees to explore "mutual interests" (other than safety and health benefits), while 75 percent contain pledges of joint effort toward overall cooperation.

Some type of quality of worklife program is found in 25 of the 400 sample contracts, a steady climb from 17 recorded in the 1986 study and nine recorded in the 1983 analysis.

*Industry pattern:* Provisions for union-management cooperation are found in 54 percent (compared to 46 percent in 1986) of manufacturing agreements and 51 percent (compared to 45 percent in 1986) of non-manufacturing contracts. From 60 percent to 83 percent of utilities, mining, primary metals, rubber, lumber, leather, furniture, maritime, transportation, and electrical machinery agreements contain cooperation clauses. Further, these provisions appear in at least one-half of communications, transportation equipment, chemicals, paper, and stone-clay-glass agreements.

# Seniority

Seniority provisions, defined as employment service credit, are found in 91 percent of contracts in the Basic Patterns database—98 percent of manufacturing contracts and 79 percent of non-manufacturing. Seniority is used most often to determine an employee's ranking for purposes of layoff (see p. 67), promotion, and transfer.

Geographic analysis reveals that seniority is discussed in from 70 percent of contracts in the Rocky Mountain region to 98 percent of contracts in the Southeast region.

In 89 percent of contracts containing seniority provisions, seniority is based entirely on the length of an employee's continuous service. Three percent of these provisions define seniority as a combination of length of service and job qualifications, such as ability and fitness.

***Probationary periods*** are required under 83 percent of sample contracts. Employees must complete these trial periods before they attain seniority rights. Of contracts requiring probationary periods, 76 percent state that the employer retains full authority to discipline or discharge employees during such time.

The most prevalent durations specified in probationary period provisions are 60 days (24 percent), 90 days (21 percent), 30 days (20 percent), 45 days (9 percent), 180 days (6 percent), and 65 days (5 percent). At the end of the trial period, an employee's seniority dates back to the date of hire.

*Industry pattern:* Probationary periods are contained in all contracts in chemicals, fabricated metals, furniture, lumber, machinery, petroleum, primary metals, and rubber. In addition, such clauses appear in at least three-fourths of sample agreements in every industry except communications, construction, insurance and finance, maritime, and printing.

### Probationary Periods
*(Frequency Expressed as Percentage of Contracts)*

|  | Provisions | 30 Days | 45 Days | 60 Days | 90 Days | 180 Days |
|---|---|---|---|---|---|---|
| All Industries | 83 | 17 | 8 | 20 | 18 | 5 |
| Manufacturing | 92 | 19 | 9 | 20 | 19 | 4 |
| Non-manufacturing | 68 | 13 | 5 | 19 | 15 | 7 |

***Loss of seniority*** is discussed in 81 percent of agreements studied—91 percent in manufacturing and 65 percent in non-manufacturing. Of these provisions, 90 percent state that seniority is lost after long-term layoff. Under contracts specifying loss of seniority after layoff, 57 percent specify that seniority is lost after a uniform length of time, and 43 percent key retention of seniority to an employee's length of service.

Reasons for loss of seniority other than lengthy layoff frequently are included in agreements. Under contracts dealing with seniority loss, 81 percent revoke seniority for failure to respond to recall; 51 percent for unauthorized absence; 45 percent for failure to report after leave of absence expiration; and 25 percent after sickness or disability leave expiration.

*Seniority lists are required* in 70 percent of contracts in the database—82 percent in manufacturing and 50 percent in non-manufacturing. Of these provisions, 44 percent specify that the lists must be posted, and 76 percent state that the union will be given copies of the lists. Management is required to revise the list periodically under 77 percent of the clauses. Twenty percent of the provisions permit the union or the employee to protest lists, most often within 30 days.

*Industry pattern:* Seniority lists are required in all contracts in furniture, machinery, petroleum, rubber, and textiles, and in at least two-thirds of the contracts in every industry except apparel, construction, insurance and finance, leather, maritime, printing, retail, services, and utilities.

### Seniority Provisions

*(Frequency Expressed as Percentage of Contracts in Each Region)*

| | Seniority Lists | Probationary Period | Loss of Seniority | Consideration of Seniority in Promotion | Consideration of Seniority in Transfer | Trial Period in New Job |
|---|---|---|---|---|---|---|
| All Regions | 70 | 83 | 81 | 74 | 59 | 55 |
| Middle Atlantic | 63 | 78 | 75 | 75 | 55 | 53 |
| Midwest | 67 | 83 | 83 | 75 | 75 | 58 |
| New England | 72 | 72 | 80 | 60 | 56 | 64 |
| North Central | 82 | 89 | 87 | 83 | 71 | 65 |
| Rocky Mountain | 40 | 70 | 70 | 50 | 40 | 50 |
| Southeast | 84 | 94 | 90 | 86 | 66 | 68 |
| Southwest | 69 | 77 | 77 | 69 | 62 | 62 |
| West Coast | 48 | 83 | 76 | 57 | 39 | 35 |
| Multiregion | 72 | 78 | 78 | 70 | 52 | 40 |

## Promotion

Seniority is assigned a role in determining promotions in 74 percent of the contracts studied—83 percent in manufacturing and 59 percent in non-manufacturing.

*Seniority is the sole factor* in promotions in 5 percent of sample agreements.

*Seniority is the determining factor* in promoting employees in 43 percent of contracts in the database. Under these provisions, the most senior employees are promoted if they are qualified for the available job.

*Seniority is a secondary factor* to be considered only when other factors are equal in 25 percent of agreements studied.

*Seniority is given equal consideration* with other factors in determining promotions in only three of the 400 samples contracts.

*Industry pattern:* Clauses specifying seniority as a factor in promotion appear in at least 60 percent of agreements in all industries except apparel, construction, maritime, and printing.

## Consideration of Seniority in Promotion

*(Frequency Expressed as Percentage of Contracts)*

|  | Applied in Some Degree | Sole Factor | Determing Factor | Secondary Factor | Equal With Other Factors |
|---|---|---|---|---|---|
| All Industries | 74 | 5 | 43 | 25 | 1 |
| Manufacturing | 83 | 5 | 50 | 27 | — |
| Non-manufacturing | 59 | 5 | 30 | 23 | 1 |

## Posting of Vacancies

Job vacancies must be posted, usually for a specified period of time, under 64 percent of contracts in the database. Posting provisions are found in 72 percent of manufacturing agreements and 52 percent of non-manufacturing contracts. Bidding procedures are included in 61 percent of sample agreements. A time limit within which bids must be submitted is specified in 68 percent of bidding clauses.

Trial periods on new jobs are called for in 55 percent of sample contracts.

*Industry pattern:* Provisions requiring that job vacancies be posted are found in at least half of the contracts in all industries except apparel, construction, maritime, printing, retail, and transportation equipment.

## Transfer

Seniority is considered in granting employees' requests for transfers under 59 percent of agreements in the database—69 percent in manufacturing contracts and 43 percent in non-manufacturing.

*Seniority is the sole factor* in granting employees' requests for transfers in only 8 percent of the sample.

*Seniority is the determining factor* in transfers under 36 percent of the contracts. Under these provisions, senior employees are permitted to transfer if they can do the job.

*Seniority is a secondary factor* in granting requests for transfers in 14 percent of agreements studied. Under these provisions, seniority is considered when other factors, such as qualifications, are equal.

*Seniority is given equal consideration* with other factors in authorizing transfers in only one percent of sample contracts.

*Industry pattern:* Seniority is considered in granting requests for transfers in at least two-thirds of contracts in communications, chemicals, electrical machinery, furniture, lumber, machinery, paper, rubber, transportation, foods, transportation equipment, primary metals, stone-clay-glass, textiles, mining, and utilities.

### Consideration of Seniority in Transfer

*(Frequency Expressed as Percentage of Contracts)*

| | Applied in Some Degree | Sole Factor | Determing Factor | Secondary Factor | Equal With Other Factors |
|---|---|---|---|---|---|
| All Industries | 59 | 8 | 36 | 14 | 1 |
| Manufacturing | 69 | 7 | 44 | 16 | 1 |
| Non-manufacturing | 43 | 8 | 23 | 11 | 1 |

*Temporary transfer provisions* appear in 56 percent of sample contracts. These clauses are found in 70 percent of manufacturing agreements and 34 percent of those in non-manufacturing. In 69 percent of these provisions, temporary transfers are determined solely by management and in 63 percent a limit on duration is imposed.

*Special transfer rights* for disabled or aged employees, no longer able to perform their regular work, are called for in 33 percent of agreements—44 percent in manufacturing and 16 percent in non-manufacturing.

## Effect of Transfers on Seniority Status

*Seniority upon transfer* from one department to another is considered in 26 percent of contracts in the database. Under 39 percent of these provisions, seniority is carried to the new department immediately, under 42 percent seniority is retained in the old department for a specified period, and under 35 percent of the clauses, seniority is carried to the new department after a time.

*Seniority upon transfer from the bargaining unit*—other than to supervisory positions—is dealt with in 43 percent of contracts studied. These provisions are found in 53 percent of manufacturing agreements and 28 percent of non-manufacturing. Of these clauses, 23 percent permit employees to retain their bargaining unit seniority indefinitely and 31 percent allow seniority to be retained for a while and then lost. Provisions for indefinite accumulation of seniority are found in 12 percent and for accumulation for a time and then lost are specified in 10 percent. Under 17 percent of these provisions, seniority may be accumulated for a time and then retained.

*Industry pattern:* Provisions dealing with the effect on an employee's seniority upon transfer out of the bargaining unit to a non-supervisory position are included in at least half of the contracts in chemicals, electrical machinery, fabricated metals, furniture, leather, machinery, mining, paper, primary metals, rubber, textiles, transportation, and transportation equipment.

## Seniority Provisions

*(Frequency Expressed as Percentage of Industry Contracts)*

| | Proba-tionary Periods | Lists Re-quired | Vacan-cies Posted | Factor In: Promo-tions | Layoffs | Trans-fers | Status Upon Transfer To: Non-bargain-ing | Super-visory Job |
|---|---|---|---|---|---|---|---|---|
| ALL INDUSTRIES | 83 | 70 | 64 | 74 | 87 | 59 | 43 | 28 |
| MANUFACTUR-ING | 92 | 82 | 72 | 83 | 95 | 69 | 53 | 38 |
| Apparel | 89 | 11 | 11 | 22 | 78 | 11 | — | — |
| Chemicals | 100 | 81 | 81 | 100 | 100 | 69 | 50 | 50 |
| Electrical Machin-ery | 75 | 75 | 75 | 90 | 95 | 70 | 60 | 35 |
| Fabricated Metals | 100 | 89 | 79 | 74 | 95 | 63 | 68 | 32 |
| Foods | 95 | 86 | 86 | 86 | 100 | 67 | 33 | 29 |
| Furniture | 100 | 100 | 83 | 67 | 100 | 67 | 50 | 50 |
| Leather | 75 | 50 | 50 | 75 | 100 | 25 | 75 | 50 |
| Lumber | 100 | 71 | 100 | 100 | 100 | 71 | 29 | 29 |
| Machinery | 100 | 100 | 92 | 88 | 100 | 88 | 77 | 46 |
| Paper | 93 | 71 | 79 | 100 | 86 | 100 | 50 | 50 |
| Petroleum | 100 | 100 | 71 | 100 | 100 | 43 | — | 43 |
| Primary Metals | 100 | 92 | 92 | 92 | 96 | 72 | 56 | 40 |
| Printing | 25 | 38 | 25 | 25 | 88 | 38 | — | — |
| Rubber | 100 | 100 | 83 | 67 | 83 | 83 | 67 | 50 |
| Stone—Clay—Glass | 92 | 69 | 77 | 92 | 92 | 69 | 46 | 31 |
| Textiles | 90 | 100 | 80 | 80 | 100 | 70 | 60 | 30 |
| Transportation Equipment | 91 | 91 | 38 | 82 | 91 | 74 | 71 | 53 |
| NON-MANUFAC-TURING | 68 | 50 | 52 | 59 | 74 | 43 | 28 | 12 |
| Communications | 70 | 90 | 80 | 70 | 100 | 70 | 30 | 30 |
| Construction | 3 | — | — | — | 10 | — | — | — |
| Insurance & Fi-nance | 71 | 57 | 86 | 86 | 71 | 14 | 43 | 14 |
| Maritime | 38 | 25 | — | 13 | 38 | 13 | 13 | 13 |
| Mining | 83 | 75 | 83 | 100 | 83 | 83 | 75 | 25 |
| Retail | 93 | 63 | 30 | 63 | 96 | 22 | 22 | — |
| Services | 93 | 37 | 70 | 67 | 96 | 48 | 22 | — |
| Transportation | 88 | 88 | 76 | 80 | 92 | 72 | 52 | 36 |
| Utilities | 80 | 40 | 100 | 100 | 90 | 100 | 30 | 10 |

## Seniority and Supervisory Jobs

Seniority status of bargaining unit employees promoted to supervisory jobs is considered in 28 percent of agreements in the database, including 38 percent in manufacturing contracts and 12 percent in non-manufacturing.

Of these provisions, 18 percent allow indefinite accumulation of seniority while outside the unit, 13 percent specify that seniority is accumulated for a limited time and then is lost, and 17 percent allow seniority to be accumulated for a time and then retained. Seniority is retained for a limited time but then is lost under 24 percent of these clauses and is lost immediately upon transfer to a supervisory job under 3 percent.

*Industry pattern:* The effect on an employee's seniority upon promotion to a supervisory position is not discussed in any construction, retail, apparel, printing, or services contracts, but is discussed in at least half of those in chemicals, furniture, leather, transportation equipment, paper, and rubber.

# 13

# Strikes and Lockouts

Strike and lockout provisions appear in 96 percent of the 400 sample agreements found in CBNC's Basic Patterns database and are somewhat more common in contracts in manufacturing industries (97 percent) than in non-manufacturing industries (93 percent). Geographic analysis shows that such clauses are contained in from 90 percent to 100 percent of contracts in areas designated in the database.

## No-strike pledges

No-strike pledges are found in 94 percent of all agreements surveyed, falling into two general categories: 1) unconditional bans on interference with production during the life of the contract; and 2) conditional bans which permit strikes under certain circumstances. A no-strike ban most commonly is lifted after exhaustion of the grievance procedure, after an arbitration award has been violated, and/or over non-compliance with a contract provision.

Unconditional strike bans appear in 62 percent of sample agreements, compared to 59 percent in 1986. Conditional bans are contained in 32 percent of contracts analyzed, down from 35 percent in 1986.

### No-Strike Pledges

*(Frequency Expressed as Percentage of Contracts)*

| | All Industries | Manu-facturing | Non-manu-facturing |
|---|---|---|---|
| Unconditional Pledges | 62 | 65 | 57 |
| Conditional Pledges Waived After: | | | |
| Exhaustion of | | | |
|   Grievance Procedure | 9 | 11 | 7 |
| Violation of Arbitration Award | 12 | 11 | 12 |
| Company Refusal to Arbitrate | 4 | 3 | 5 |
| Non-compliance With | | | |
|   Portion of Contract | 8 | 4 | 15 |
| Reopener Impasse | 4 | 3 | 4 |
| Issues Outside | | | |
|   Grievance Procedure | 2 | 3 | 1 |
| Other | 9 | 7 | 12 |

*Industry pattern:* No-strike pledges are found in 96 percent of manufacturing contracts and in 90 percent of non-manufacturing agreements. All contracts in 12 industries include a no-strike pledge—textiles, petroleum, apparel, lumber, furniture, paper, leather, rubber, electrical machinery, maritime, foods, and utilities. Three-quarters or more of contracts in every other industry have such a provision, with the exception of printing (50 percent).

**Unconditional pledges** are found in one-half or more of the contracts in 19 industries, appearing in three-quarters or more of agreements in paper and leather (each 100 percent); lumber and insurance and finance (each 86 percent); furniture (83 percent); machinery (81 percent); utilities (80 percent); stone-clay-glass (77 percent); primary metals (76 percent); and mining (75 percent).

**Conditional no-strike pledges** are found in 35 percent of non-manufacturing agreements and in 29 percent of manufacturing agreements. These clauses appear in one-half or more of contracts in construction (83 percent), apparel (78 percent), petroleum (71 percent), textiles (60 percent), and electrical machinery (55 percent). No-strike bans may be lifted for the following reasons:

*Exhaustion of grievance procedure:* Twenty-nine percent of conditional bans are lifted for this reason. The waiver is found in a majority of industries, but mainly in primary metals, transportation, electrical machinery, transportation equipment, chemicals, construction, printing, and utilities.

*Violation of arbitration award:* No-strike bans lifted for this reason are found in 37 percent of sample contracts with conditional bans. This waiver appears most often in apparel, electrical machinery, construction, communications, foods, retail, services, and transportation.

*Company refusal to arbitrate dispute:* Eleven percent of the contracts with conditional bans allow strikes in this situation. Ten of the 26 industries studied have at least one contract with such a provision, but no industry has a concentration.

*Non-compliance with portion of agreement:* Twenty-six percent of conditional bans are lifted for this reason. Eleven industries have at least one contract with such a clause, but the provision is concentrated in contracts in only two industries—apparel (56 percent) and construction (55 percent).

*Deadlocked contract reopener:* Strikes are permitted in this circumstance in 11 percent of contracts with conditional no-strike pledges, occurring most frequently in the textiles (30 percent), petroleum (29 percent), and maritime (25 percent) industries.

*Issues outside grievance procedure:* Only 6 percent of conditional bans are waived for this reason.

## Strike and Lockout Provisions

*(Frequency Expressed as Percentage of Contracts in Each Region)*

| | Middle Atlantic | Midwest | New England | North Central | Rocky Mountain | Southeast | Southwest | West Coast | Multiregion |
|---|---|---|---|---|---|---|---|---|---|
| Provisions | 96 | 92 | 92 | 97 | 90 | 98 | 100 | 98 | 92 |
| No Strike Pledge | 94 | 88 | 92 | 94 | 90 | 94 | 100 | 96 | 92 |
| Unconditional | 65 | 63 | 60 | 69 | 50 | 70 | 46 | 63 | 47 |
| Conditional | 29 | 25 | 32 | 26 | 40 | 24 | 54 | 33 | 45 |
| No Lockout Pledge | 88 | 88 | 84 | 89 | 90 | 90 | 92 | 85 | 88 |
| Unconditional | 69 | 71 | 72 | 72 | 80 | 78 | 62 | 63 | 57 |
| Conditional | 21 | 17 | 12 | 16 | 10 | 12 | 31 | 22 | 32 |
| Union Strike Liability | 33 | 38 | 56 | 49 | 20 | 64 | 31 | 11 | 45 |
| Definition of Authorized Strike | 6 | 13 | 8 | 10 | 10 | 8 | — | 4 | 17 |
| Penalties for Strikers | 33 | 42 | — | 51 | 20 | 66 | 31 | 24 | 43 |
| Other Employees Access to Plant During Strike | 4 | 4 | 4 | 2 | 10 | 6 | 15 | 4 | 5 |
| Non-Striking Employees May Observe Picket Line | 21 | 29 | 24 | 17 | 60 | 18 | 23 | 59 | 23 |
| Struck Work Provisions | 6 | — | 4 | 8 | — | 6 | — | 15 | 8 |

## No-Lockout Pledges

No-lockout pledges appear in 88 percent of contracts in the database. These provisions usually contain language similar, if not identical, to that found in no-strike pledges. The frequency of unconditional pledges rose from 66 percent in 1986 to 69 percent; conditional bans decreased from 24 percent in 1986 to 20 percent.

*Industry pattern:* No-lockout pledges appear in 91 percent of manufacturing agreements and in 83 percent of non-manufacturing contracts. All textiles, apparel, lumber, furniture, paper, maritime, petroleum, electrical machinery, leather, and rubber agreements contain no-lockout pledges. In addition, they appear in at least three-fourths of all contracts in every other industry, with the exception of communications (70 percent), transportation (56 percent), and printing (25 percent).

## No-Lockout Pledges

*(Frequency Expressed as Percentage of Contracts)*

| | All Industries | Manu-facturing | Non-manu-facturing |
|---|---|---|---|
| Unconditional Pledges | 69 | 72 | 63 |
| Conditional Pledges Waived After: | | | |
| Exhaustion of | | | |
| Grievance Procedure | 8 | 9 | 7 |
| Violation of Arbitration Award | 7 | 6 | 8 |
| Union Refusal to Arbitrate | 3 | 2 | 5 |
| Non-compliance With | | | |
| Portion of Contract | 3 | 2 | 3 |
| Reopener Impasse | 1 | 1 | 1 |
| Other | 4 | 2 | 6 |

***Unconditional bans*** appear in all contracts in paper, rubber, leather, and maritime. Such provisions are found in one-half or more of agreements in every other industry except construction, transportation, printing, and communications.

***Conditional no-lockout pledges,*** appearing in 19 percent of manufacturing contracts and 21 percent of non-manufacturing contracts, may be waived for reasons similar to those that permit waiver of no-strike pledges, including the following:

*Exhaustion of grievance procedure:* This is the reason for waiver of the no-lockout pledge in 42 percent of contracts with such a provision. It is found in at least one contract in 12 of the 26 industries and occurs with greatest frequency in transportation equipment (24 percent) and transportation and electrical machinery (each 20 percent) contracts.

*Violation of arbitration award:* Thirty-six percent of conditional bans may be waived for this reason. This waiver most often appears in agreements in communications (20 percent), foods (24 percent), and electrical machinery (25 percent).

*Union refusal to arbitrate dispute:* Lockouts are allowed in this circumstance under 14 percent of contracts with conditional pledges. No single industry has a significant number of agreements with such a clause.

*Non-compliance with portion of agreement:* No-lockout bans are lifted for this reason in 14 percent of contracts with conditional pledges. Such provisions are not concentrated in any one industry.

*Deadlocked contract reopener:* Six percent of conditional bans may be waived for this reason. One industry, textiles, has the greatest concentration (20 percent).

Waivers for various other reasons appear in 21 percent of contracts with conditional no-lockout pledges.

## Limitations on Union Liability

Provisions limiting a union's liability for violation of a no-strike pledge appear in 41 percent of agrements studied. Some form of positive action usually is required of the union to avoid liability. Of contracts with liability clauses, 77 percent require that the union attempt to get the employees to return to work and 27 percent specify that the union must publicly disavow the strike. Twenty-seven percent of the provisions deny release of union liability if the work stoppage was initiated or encouraged by any union officer. Various other requirements of the union are found in 23 percent of these clauses. Further, many contracts specify more than one requirement of the union.

Some agreements approach the question of liability by specifying conditions under which a strike is authorized. Such statements appear in 9 percent of the sample and are more commonly found in manufacturing (11 percent) than in non-manufacturing (5 percent) agreements. Of these, 50 percent indicate who may or may not authorize a strike and 75 percent require approval from the international union.

The local union is exempt from responsibility for unauthorized strikes in 73 percent of liability clauses; the international union is exempt in 32 percent.

### Union Avoidance of Strike Liability

*(Frequency Expressed as Percentage of Contracts)*

|  | All Industries | Manu-facturing | Non-manu-facturing |
|---|---|---|---|
| Liability Limited | 41 | 49 | 28 |
| Requirements Placed on Union: |  |  |  |
| Strike Not Initiated by Officers | 11 | 13 | 9 |
| Must Order Work Resumed | 32 | 38 | 23 |
| Must Disavow Strike | 11 | 12 | 9 |
| Other | 9 | 9 | 10 |

*Industry pattern:* Provisions limiting union liability are far more common in manufacturing (49 percent) than in non-manufacturing (28 percent) agreements. Such clauses appear in all textiles agreements and in one-half or more of those in apparel, furniture, fabricated metals, leather, stone-clay-glass, paper, insurance and finance, utilities, rubber, and chemicals.

## Penalties for Strikers

Discipline or discharge of employees participating in illegal strikes is permitted in 42 percent of agreements in the sample database. Of these, 40 percent provide for appeal from the penalty imposed, although 52 percent of agreements permitting appeal limit it to the question of participation in the strike.

*Industry pattern:* Provisions allowing penalties for illegal strikes are far more common in manufacturing (52 percent) than in non-manufacturing (26 percent) contracts. All furniture, rubber and textiles agreements contain such a provision. One-half or more of the contracts in eight other industries—transportation equipment (68 percent), paper (57 percent), apparel and primary metals (each 56 percent), machinery (54 percent), and mining, utilities, and leather (each 50 percent)—have such clauses.

## Clauses Limiting Union Strike Liability

*(Frequency Expressed as Percentage of Industry Contracts)*

|  | Year | | | | |
|---|---|---|---|---|---|
|  | 1975 | 1979 | 1983 | 1986 | 1989 |
| ALL INDUSTRIES | 43 | 35 | 37 | 39 | 41 |
| MANUFACTURING | 51 | 42 | 44 | 47 | 49 |
| Apparel | 67 | 78 | 78 | 89 | 89 |
| Chemicals | 50 | 56 | 44 | 44 | 50 |
| Electrical Machinery | 50 | 35 | 35 | 35 | 40 |
| Fabricated Metals | 47 | 32 | 53 | 53 | 53 |
| Foods | 52 | 24 | 33 | 29 | 38 |
| Furniture | 100 | 83 | 67 | 83 | 83 |
| Leather | 75 | 75 | 75 | 50 | 75 |
| Lumber | 29 | 29 | 29 | 43 | 43 |
| Machinery | 45 | 40 | 48 | 48 | 42 |
| Paper | 50 | 50 | 57 | 57 | 57 |
| Petroleum | 14 | 14 | 14 | 14 | 14 |
| Primary Metals | 40 | 32 | 24 | 28 | 40 |
| Printing | 13 | 13 | 13 | 13 | 13 |
| Rubber | 83 | 85 | 83 | 100 | 83 |
| Stone, Clay, & Glass | 62 | 46 | 62 | 69 | 62 |
| Textiles | 100 | 100 | 100 | 100 | 100 |
| Transportation Equipment | 26 | 29 | 29 | 37 | 38 |
| NON-MANUFACTURING | 26 | 25 | 25 | 27 | 28 |
| Communications | 22 | 10 | 10 | 10 | 10 |
| Construction | 29 | 24 | 17 | 21 | 24 |
| Insurance & Finance | 67 | 71 | 57 | 71 | 71 |
| Maritime | 13 | — | — | 13 | 13 |
| Mining | 58 | 58 | 67 | 58 | 42 |
| Retail | 11 | 26 | 30 | 33 | 22 |
| Services | — | 11 | 19 | 22 | 30 |
| Transportation | 16 | 16 | 8 | 8 | 20 |
| Utilities | 60 | 50 | 50 | 50 | 50 |

**Appeals are permitted** in 42 percent of manufacturing agreements containing penalty provisions and in 33 percent of non-manufacturing contracts with such clauses. These provisions are most common in contracts in furniture (83 percent) and textiles (80 percent), and are found in one-fourth or more of the agreements in electrical machinery, transportation equipment, leather, paper, and transportation.

## Picket Lines and Struck Work _____

Twenty-six percent of contracts studied state that employees may observe picket lines in certain situations. As a general rule, picket lines must be primary and legal to be considered within the purview of such provisions. Of agreements with such clauses, 10 percent allow observance of a picket line only at the employees' own plant; 66 percent allow observance at any plant; and 24 percent allow observance if certain other conditions are met, such as approval of the strike by the local central labor body. Nine percent of contracts containing picket line provisions permit observance only if the line is manned by the employees' own union.

Provisions allowing observance of picket lines are far more common in non-manufacturing (45 percent) than in manufacturing (14 percent) contracts. Picket line clauses are found in 74 percent of contracts in retail, 67 percent in apparel, 63 percent each in maritime and printing, 60 percent in communications, 59 percent in construction, and 48 percent in services.

*Struck-work clauses* appear in 7 percent of the sample, and in 7 percent each in manufacturing and non-manufacturing agreements. Of the 28 contracts containing struck-work provisions, 16 allow employees to refuse to handle only goods struck by their own union, while 12 permit employees to refuse to handle any struck goods. Employer pledges not to accept struck goods are found in only six of the sample contracts.

*Access to the plant* during a strike by non-striking employees is guaranteed in 5 percent of agreements included in the database. Such guarantees most often apply to maintenance and security personnel.

_____

# 14

# Union Security

Union security provisions, including check-off and hiring arrangements, are found in all but two of the agreements contained in the Basic Patterns database. Geographic analysis shows that such clauses are contained in from 98 to 100 percent of contracts in regions designated in the database.

Eighty-three percent of the contracts analyzed provide for one or more of the principal forms of union security—union shop, modified union shop, maintenance-of-membership, and agency shop. Check-off provisions appear in 91 percent of the sample; hiring provisions in 22 percent.

**Union shop** is by far the most prevalent form of security. Provided in 62 percent of the sample, union shop clauses require that all employees in the bargaining unit become members and maintain membership as a condition of employment.

*Industry pattern:* At least three-fourths of contracts in apparel, construction, furniture, printing, retail, and rubber contain union shop provisions. Such provisions are absent in petroleum agreements analyzed and appear in less than 50 percent of those in primary metals (48 percent), lumber (43 percent), utilities (40 percent), communications and textiles (each 30 percent), and mining (17 percent).

**Modified union shop** provisions are found in 13 percent of sample agreements. Of the various forms of modification, the most common requires union membership of all employees except those who were not members on or before the contract's effective date or another specified date. In a few agreements, groups such as temporary workers and religious objectors are excused from the membership requirement.

*Industry pattern:* Modified union shop provisions are found in 28 percent of primary metals agreements, 25 percent of mining, 24 percent of foods, and 20 percent each of electrical machinery and utilities. This type of provision does not appear in any leather, lumber, printing, furniture, rubber, or textiles industries agreements studied.

**Agency shop,** which requires payment of service fees—usually equal in amount to union dues—by employees who choose not to join the union, is found in 11 percent of contracts analyzed. In 5 percent of the sample, agency shop exists as the sole form of union security. The remaining 6 percent of agency shop provisions are found in contracts covering multistate operations—almost three-fourths (73 percent) appear in combination with union shop and the other more than one-fourth (27 percent) with modified union shop. In such instances, agency shop is applicable, to the extent that it is lawful, in states that prohibit compulsory union membership.

*Industry pattern:* Agency shop provisions (as the sole form of union security) appear in 40 percent of communications, 17 percent of furniture, 16 percent of transportation, 13 percent of maritime industry contracts, and in

10 percent each of electrical machinery and utilities agreements in the database.

## Union Security Provisions

*(Frequency Expressed as Percentage of Contracts)*

| | Union Shop | Modi-fied Union Shop | Agency Shop Only | Main-tenance of Member-ship | Hiring | Check-off |
|---|---|---|---|---|---|---|
| ALL INDUSTRIES | 62 | 13 | 5 | 4 | 22 | 91 |
| MANUFACTURING | 60 | 14 | 4 | 4 | 8 | 96 |
| Apparel | 89 | 11 | — | — | 33 | 89 |
| Chemicals | 50 | 19 | — | 13 | 6 | 94 |
| Electrical Machinery | 60 | 20 | 10 | 5 | 5 | 100 |
| Fabricated Metals | 58 | 16 | 5 | 11 | 5 | 95 |
| Foods | 57 | 24 | 5 | — | 14 | 95 |
| Furniture | 83 | — | 17 | — | — | 100 |
| Leather | 50 | — | — | — | — | 100 |
| Lumber | 43 | — | — | — | — | 100 |
| Machinery | 73 | 19 | 4 | — | — | 100 |
| Paper | 57 | 14 | — | 7 | — | 93 |
| Petroleum | — | 14 | — | 14 | 14 | 100 |
| Primary Metals | 48 | 28 | 4 | 4 | — | 100 |
| Printing | 88 | — | — | — | 63 | 63 |
| Rubber | 83 | — | — | — | — | 100 |
| Stone, Clay, & Glass | 69 | 15 | — | — | 8 | 100 |
| Textiles | 30 | — | — | 10 | — | 90 |
| Transportation Equipment | 68 | 3 | 6 | 3 | 9 | 97 |
| NON-MANUFACTURING | 64 | 12 | 8 | 3 | 45 | 84 |
| Communications | 30 | 10 | 40 | — | 20 | 100 |
| Construction | 79 | 10 | — | — | 90 | 55 |
| Insurance & Finance | 57 | 14 | — | 14 | — | 100 |
| Maritime | 63 | 13 | 13 | 13 | 100 | 50 |
| Mining | 17 | 25 | — | — | — | 100 |
| Retail | 89 | 7 | 4 | — | 44 | 74 |
| Services | 74 | 4 | 7 | 7 | 56 | 96 |
| Transportation | 56 | 16 | 16 | — | 16 | 100 |
| Utilities | 40 | 20 | 10 | 10 | 30 | 100 |

*Maintenance-of-membership* provisions, requiring present union members to so remain but imposing no obligation on non-members, appear in only 4 percent of sample agreements.

*Industry pattern:* Maintenance-of-membership provisions are found in 14 percent each of petroleum and insurance and finance contracts, 13 percent each of chemicals and maritime agreements, and in at least 10 percent of fabricated metals, textiles, and utilities agreements.

*Right-to-work laws,* prohibiting compulsory union membership (in effect in 21 states), influence union security provisions in 27 percent of contracts in the database. Fifteen percent of contracts analyzed cover bargaining units located wholly in right-to-work states; the other 12 percent cover multistate units, some of which are located in right-to-work states. Further, 5 percent of the contracts surveyed either call for a first union security provision or a stronger provision than that already appearing in the contract should right-to-work or other limiting laws be repealed.

Because of the legal restrictions in many states, a geographic analysis reveals wide variations in the frequency of union shop provisions. Inclusion of these clauses ranges from 15 percent in the Southwest region and 16 percent in the Southeast region, to 90 percent in the Rocky Mountain area. Check-off provisions, on the other hand, are prevalent in all regions and range from 67 percent of West Coast contracts to 100 percent of Rocky Mountain agreements.

## Union Security Provisions

*(Frequency Expressed as Percentage of Contracts in Each Region)*

|  | Union Shop | Modified Union Shop | Agency Shop Only | Main-tenance of Member-ship | Hiring | Check-off |
|---|---|---|---|---|---|---|
| All Regions | 62 | 13 | 5 | 4 | 22 | 91 |
| Middle Atlantic | 71 | 18 | 4 | 4 | 23 | 96 |
| Midwest | 67 | 8 | – | 4 | 21 | 83 |
| New England | 72 | 24 | 4 | – | 32 | 92 |
| North Central | 67 | 15 | 8 | 5 | 8 | 96 |
| Rocky Mountain | 90 | – | – | – | 30 | 100 |
| Southeast | 16 | – | 2 | 8 | 14 | 96 |
| Southwest | 15 | 8 | – | – | 31 | 85 |
| West Coast | 78 | 13 | 9 | 2 | 54 | 67 |
| Multiregion | 63 | 17 | 10 | 3 | 20 | 95 |

## Hiring Arrangements

Hiring provisions are found in 22 percent of contracts in the database—8 percent in manufacturing and 45 percent in non-manufacturing.

*Industry pattern:* Hiring provisions are found in all maritime agreements analyzed, and in 90 percent of construction, 63 percent of printing, 56 percent of services, 44 percent of retail, and in at least 30 percent of apparel and utilities agreements.

**Hiring-preference provisions,** requiring that preference in employment be given to workers in the area and/or to those with experience in the industry, are found in 36 percent of contracts with hiring provisions, or in 8 percent of the entire sample.

*Industry pattern:* Provisions for preference in hiring are most common in construction (55 percent) and maritime and printing (each 25 percent) contracts. Such clauses also appear in at least 10 percent of apparel, communications, utilities, services, and foods industry agreements.

*Hiring procedures,* referring to a union role in furnishing candidates for employment, are found in 20 percent of the database—7 percent in manufacturing and 42 percent in non-manufacturing. Of these provisions, 93 percent call for union operation of a hiring hall; the remainder call for a joint labor-management operation. In many cases, however, the employer may seek job applicants from other sources either simultaneously or after the union has been given the first opportunity to supply candidates.

*Industry pattern:* Provisions for hiring halls are found in 90 percent of construction, 88 percent of maritime, 63 percent of printing, 56 percent of services, 41 percent of retail, and in 33 percent of apparel agreements.

## Check-off

Provisions for check-off are contained in 91 percent of contracts studied—96 percent of manufacturing and 84 percent of non-manufacturing agreements.

*Industry pattern:* Check-off provisions appear in all contracts in the communications, electrical machinery, furniture, insurance and finance, leather, lumber, machinery, mining, petroleum, primary metals, rubber, stone-clay-glass, transportation, and utilities industries. Further, these provisions are found in at least 50 percent of contracts in all other industries analyzed.

*Items to be deducted* are specified in all contracts containing check-off provisions. Of these agreements, only one does not mention union dues as an item to be deducted; 72 percent mention initiation fees; 25 percent mention assessments; 21 percent mention politicfal action contributions; and 18 percent mention other fees such as reinstatement and/or agency fees. A contract may provide for only one type of deduction or may permit a combination of the specified deductions.

*Amounts to be deducted* are referred to in 10 percent of contracts containing check-off provisions. Of these, more three-fourths (78 percent) specify a fixed amount of dues to be deducted, and the other 22 percent place limitations on deductions.

*Revocation of check-off authorization* is mentioned in 51 percent of sample agreements providing for check-off. Of these, 81 percent hold authorizations to be irrevocable for the term of the contract or one year, whichever is shorter, and 16 percent allow employees to revoke at any time or upon short notice.

*Automatic renewal of check-off authorization* takes place if an employee fails to cancel under 74 percent of irrevocable check-off provisions. In 95 percent of these cases, the renewed authorization continues to be irrevocable for specified periods, and in the other 5 percent it continues on a revocable basis. Authorizations revocable from the outset remain in effect until cancelled; therefore renewal problems do not arise.

*Escape periods,* during which resignation from check-off and/or union membership is permitted, are specified in 29 percent of sample agreements—38 percent in manufacturing and 14 percent in non-manufacturing. These provisions are found in 83 percent of rubber contracts, and in at least 50 percent of chemicals, paper, textiles, and transportation equipment agreements.

## Frequency of Check-off Provisions

*(Frequency Expressed as Number of Contracts)*

|  | All Industries | Manu-facturing | Non-manu-facturing |
|---|---|---|---|
| Provision for Authorized Check-off | 365 | 235 | 130 |
| Type of Authorization: |  |  |  |
| Revocable at Will | 29 | 11 | 18 |
| Irrevocable for Contract Term or One Year | 149 | 114 | 35 |
| Automatic Renewal* |  |  |  |
| Becomes Revocable | 5 | 4 | 1 |
| Continues Irrevocable | 104 | 88 | 16 |
| Deductions in Addition to Dues |  |  |  |
| Assessments | 92 | 57 | 35 |
| Initiation Fees | 262 | 192 | 70 |
| Political Action Contributions | 77 | 47 | 30 |

*After "escape" period.

# Vacations

Vacation provisions are found in 92 percent of all 400 contracts in CBNC's Basic Patterns database, and in 98 percent of all agreements outside the construction industry. Geographical analysis shows that such provisions are contained in from 70 to 98 percent of contracts in areas designated in the database.

Vacation provisions are absent in all but one construction agreement and in only six contracts in all other industries—four in maritime, and one each in apparel and transportation equipment.

## Amount of Vacation

The latest survey reveals no change since the 1986 study in the percentage of sample contracts providing one, two, or three weeks of vacation, and only a slight increase in the percentage providing four weeks. One-week vacations are less frequent than two-, three-, and four-week vacations because a number of contracts provide minimum vacations of two weeks or longer.

Five-week vacations appear in a majority of sample contracts, having risen in frequency from only 2 percent in the 1966 study to 62 percent in the 1986 analysis before tapering off to 61 percent in this year's survey. Six-week vacations have climbed steadily, increasing from 5 percent in the 1971 study to 22 percent in the 1986 survey, before plateauing to 21 percent in this year's analysis.

## Trend in Amount of Vacation Per Year

*(Frequency Expressed as Percentage of Contracts)*

|             | 1961 | 1966 | 1971 | 1975 | 1979 | 1983 | 1986 | 1989 |
|-------------|------|------|------|------|------|------|------|------|
| Three weeks | 78   | 84   | 86   | 85   | 86   | 87   | 89   | 89   |
| Four weeks  | 32   | 50   | 73   | 76   | 79   | 83   | 84   | 85   |
| Five weeks  | —    | 2    | 22   | 42   | 53   | 58   | 62   | 61   |
| Six weeks   | —    | —    | 5    | 10   | 16   | 20   | 22   | 21   |

*Industry pattern:* Vacations of up to six weeks are more prevalent in manufacturing than non-manufacturing principally because of the absence of vacation provisions in all but one construction contract. Vacations of more than six weeks, however, are slightly more prevalent in non-manufacturing. Four weeks is the maximum amount of vacation in apparel contracts.

Five weeks vacation is provided in all contracts in communications, paper, petroleum, rubber, and utilities and appears in more than two-thirds of contracts in 8 other industries: chemicals, electrical machinery, fabricated metals, foods, machinery, primary metals, retail, and transportation. Chemicals, maritime, paper, petroleum, rubber, transportation, and utilities are the only industries in which at least half of contracts grant six-week vacations.

Annual vacations of more than six weeks appear in only 11 contracts—five in transportation, two each in foods and paper, and one each in communications and utilities.

### Amount of Vacation

*(Frequency Expressed as Percentage of Industry Contracts; Excludes Vacations Not Based on Length of Service)*

| | Percent of contracts providing vacations totaling: | | | | | | |
|---|---|---|---|---|---|---|---|
| | 1 week | 2 weeks | 3 weeks | 4 weeks | 5 weeks | 6 weeks | more than 6 weeks |
| ALL INDUSTRIES | 72 | 89 | 89 | 85 | 61 | 21 | 3 |
| MANUFACTURING | 79 | 97 | 97 | 93 | 66 | 22 | 2 |
| Apparel | 33 | 89 | 78 | 44 | — | — | — |
| Chemicals | 81 | 100 | 100 | 100 | 94 | 56 | — |
| Electrical Machinery | 85 | 95 | 100 | 100 | 85 | 10 | — |
| Fabricated Metals | 89 | 100 | 100 | 100 | 79 | 16 | — |
| Foods | 90 | 100 | 100 | 100 | 86 | 29 | 10 |
| Furniture | 100 | 100 | 100 | 100 | 50 | — | — |
| Leather | 100 | 100 | 100 | 100 | 25 | 25 | — |
| Lumber | 100 | 100 | 100 | 86 | 43 | 14 | — |
| Machinery | 85 | 96 | 100 | 100 | 69 | 8 | — |
| Paper | 100 | 100 | 100 | 100 | 100 | 100 | 14 |
| Petroleum | 14 | 100 | 100 | 100 | 100 | 100 | — |
| Primary Metals | 84 | 96 | 96 | 88 | 72 | — | — |
| Printing | 63 | 88 | 88 | 100 | 25 | — | — |
| Rubber | 33 | 100 | 100 | 100 | 100 | 100 | — |
| Stone, Clay & Glass | 100 | 100 | 100 | 85 | 54 | 8 | — |
| Textiles | 90 | 100 | 100 | 90 | 40 | — | — |
| Transportation Equipment | 59 | 91 | 91 | 85 | 41 | 9 | — |
| NON-MANUFACTURING | 62 | 76 | 76 | 72 | 53 | 19 | 5 |
| Communications | 90 | 90 | 100 | 100 | 100 | 10 | 10 |
| Construction | — | — | — | — | — | — | — |
| Insurance & Finance | 86 | 100 | 100 | 100 | 57 | 14 | — |
| Maritime | 50 | 50 | 50 | 38 | 38 | 50 | — |
| Mining | 50 | 92 | 83 | 75 | 58 | — | — |
| Retail | 93 | 100 | 100 | 96 | 74 | 15 | — |
| Services | 70 | 93 | 93 | 85 | 22 | — | — |
| Transportation | 80 | 100 | 96 | 96 | 88 | 56 | 20 |
| Utilities | 70 | 100 | 100 | 100 | 100 | 60 | 10 |

## Amount of Vacation

*(Frequency Expressed as Percentage of Contracts in Each Region;  Excludes Vacations Not Based on Length of Service)*

| | Percent of contracts providing vacations totaling: | | | | | | |
|---|---|---|---|---|---|---|---|
| | 1 week | 2 weeks | 3 weeks | 4 weeks | 5 weeks | 6 weeks | more than 6 weeks |
| ALL REGIONS | 72 | 89 | 89 | 85 | 61 | 21 | 3 |
| Middle Atlantic | 72 | 90 | 88 | 84 | 59 | 15 | 1 |
| Midwest | 79 | 88 | 92 | 92 | 54 | 13 | 4 |
| New England | 88 | 88 | 84 | 80 | 64 | 20 | 4 |
| North Central | 83 | 93 | 94 | 91 | 71 | 26 | 1 |
| Rocky Mountain | 50 | 70 | 70 | 60 | 30 | 20 | — |
| Southeast | 76 | 96 | 96 | 90 | 64 | 26 | 2 |
| Southwest | 46 | 77 | 69 | 69 | 54 | 23 | — |
| West Coast | 57 | 80 | 80 | 76 | 41 | 17 | — |
| Multiregion | 65 | 87 | 90 | 87 | 70 | 27 | 10 |

## Vacation Based on Length of Service

Vacation entitlement is keyed to length of service under 90 percent of sample contracts in the database. The remaining two percent of contracts mentioning vacation either grant a standard amount of vacation to all employees regardless of service or spell out the amount of vacation pay but not the amount of vacation.

The median service requirement for specified amounts of vacation in the current survey is one year for one week, two years for two weeks, eight years for three weeks, 15 years for four weeks, 21 years for five weeks, and 25 years for six weeks.

*One-week vacations* are called for in 72 percent of the total sample. Thirty-one percent of these provisions grant a vacation to employees with less than one year of service, while 69 percent require one full year of service. A week after less than one year is more common in non-manufacturing (38 percent) than in manufacturing (28 percent). Half or more of the contracts in communications, insurance and finance, maritime, printing, and utilities provide a week of vacation after less than one year of service.

*Two-week vacations* appear in 89 percent of contracts analyzed. Of these provisions, 9 percent require less than one year of service; 27 percent require one year. A majority of contracts in apparel, communications, insurance and finance, petroleum, printing, rubber, transportation, and utilities grant two weeks after a year or less of service.

Two years of service is the requirement for two-week vacations in 28 percent of two-week provisions. At least half of contracts in chemicals, foods, leather, and services specify two years of service.

Three years of service is the requirement in 27 percent of two-week provisions, appearing in at least half the agreements in fabricated metals, furniture, paper, and primary metals.

Four or five years of service are required in 9 percent of two-week provisions and are found more often in manufacturing (12 percent) than nonmanufacturing (3 percent) agreements. A five-year requirement is found most frequently in the textiles industry.

*Three-week vacations* appear in 89 percent of the agreements. Nine percent of these provisions require less than five years of service; 25 percent require five years. All contracts in petroleum and more than half of those in chemicals, rubber, and transportation require five years of service.

Six to nine years is the most common requirement, appearing in 32 percent of contracts providing three weeks of vacation. More than half of all agreements in communications, paper, electrical machinery, and utilities require six to nine years for three weeks of vacation.

Ten years is the service requirement under 28 percent of three-week provisions and is found in a majority of furniture, leather, and primary metals agreements.

Seven percent of three-week provisions require 11 or more years of service.

*Four-week vacations* are provided under 85 percent of the database sample contracts, with service requirements ranging from one to 30 years. A requirement of less than 10 years appears in 6 percent of the provisions; a requirement of 10 years appears in 12 percent. All contracts in petroleum, the only industry with a majority, provide four weeks after 10 years. Fifteen percent of four-week provisions require 11 to 14 years of service.

A 15-year service requirement appears in 31 percent of contracts providing four-week vacations, including all rubber agreements and at least half of those in communications, electrical machinery, insurance and finance, and utilities. A requirement of 16 to 19 years is found in 14 percent of these clauses and appears most frequently in mining and primary metals agreements.

Twenty years is the requirement in 19 percent of the four-week provisions, and 25 years is the requirement in 3 percent.

*Five-week vacations* appear in 61 percent of the contracts surveyed, and service requirements range from seven to 30 years. Five weeks are granted after less than 20 years in 15 percent of the provisions, while 20 years is the requirement in 34 percent. All petroleum agreements, and at least half of chemicals, retail, and rubber contracts, require 20 years for five weeks. Twenty-one to 24 years of service is required under 8 percent of five-week provisions.

Twenty-five years is the requirement under 39 percent of provisions granting five weeks of vacation. A 25-year service requirement is found in at least half of communications, insurance and finance, machinery, and primary metals agreements. Thirty years of service is required under 3 percent of five-week provisions.

*Six-week vacations* are provided in 21 percent of sample contracts. Of these provisions, 37 percent call for 30 years of service, 34 percent require 25 years, and the remainder require from 8 to 35 years. All paper, petroleum, and rubber contracts provide six weeks of vacation. At least half of chemicals, maritime, transportation, and utilities contracts grant six-week vacations. Thirty years is the most common service requirement in chemicals, petroleum, and utilities; 25 years is the most common in foods and paper.

### Vacation Service Requirements

*(Frequency Expressed as Percentage of Contracts Granting Specified Amounts of Vacation\*)*

| | Amount of Vacation | | | | | |
|---|---|---|---|---|---|---|
| Service requirement | 1 week | 2 weeks | 3 weeks | 4 weeks | 5 weeks | 6 weeks |
| Less than 1 year | 31 | 9 | 1 | — | — | — |
| 1 year | 69 | 27 | 4 | — | — | — |
| 2 years | — | 28 | 2 | — | — | — |
| 3-4 years | — | 29 | 3 | 2 | — | — |
| 5 years | — | 7 | 25 | 2 | — | — |
| 6-9 years | — | — | 32 | 2 | 1 | 2 |
| 10 years | — | — | 28 | 12 | 1 | — |
| 11-14 years | — | — | 1 | 15 | 1 | 4 |
| 15 years | — | — | 5 | 31 | 5 | 2 |
| 16-19 years | — | — | — | 14 | 7 | — |
| 20 years | — | — | — | 19 | 34 | 5 |
| 21-24 years | — | — | — | — | 8 | 5 |
| 25 years | — | — | — | 3 | 39 | 34 |
| 26-29 years | — | — | — | — | — | 9 |
| 30 years | — | — | — | — | 3 | 37 |
| 31-34 years | — | — | — | — | — | — |
| 35 years | — | — | — | — | — | 2 |

\* Because of rounding sums may not total 100.

## Two-Tier Vacation Benefits _____

Sixteen of the sample contracts in the 1989 survey provide reduced vacation benefits for new hires, up from four contracts analyzed in 1986.

Under these provisions, new employees never gain eligibility for the maximum amount granted to senior workers, or are subjected to protracted length of service requirements to achieve maximum vacation benefits.

Twelve manufacturing agreements and four non-manufacturing agreements have two-tier vacation provisions.

## Partial and Interim Benefits

In addition to vacations in weekly periods, partial vacations for employees who do not qualify for a first full vacation are called for in 20 percent of the sample. Further, interim benefits for those between weeks of qualification are provided by 29 percent of the contracts. Interim benefits often consist of additional individual days of vacation or a higher rate of vacation pay.

Partial vacations are found in 22 percent of manufacturing agreements and 16 percent of non-manufacturing contracts. Interim benefits appear in 35 percent of manufacturing and 19 percent of non-manufacturing agreements. At least half of agreements in electrical machinery, furniture, transportation equipment, and utilities provide interim benefits.

## Extended Vacations

Extended vacations appear in six of the 400 sample contracts, down from 10 in 1986 and 17 in 1983. The decline is largely due to elimination of extended vacation provisions in contracts negotiated by the United Steelworkers. Two provisions in the 1989 survey are in fabricated metals, and one each in chemicals, communications, textiles, and utilities.

The interval between extended vacations is four years in one plan and five years in the other five. The amount of vacation ranges from one week to 13 weeks.

## Vacation Pay

Eighty-seven percent of database sample contracts state the basis on which vacation pay is to be computed. Half of these provide pay at base or straight time rates; 33 percent compute pay on an employee's average earnings, usually over the previous year; 8 percent compute pay on base rates or average earnings, depending on classification; and another 8 percent compute pay on rates or averages, whichever is greater.

Inclusion of shift differentials in the computation of vacation pay is expressly called for under 22 percent of vacation pay provisions, while inclusion of overtime earnings is specified by 4 percent. In addition, many agreements basing vacation pay on average earnings state that vacation pay is a percentage of "all earnings."

Vacation bonus provisions appear in 6 percent of the sample. Some call for a flat vacation bonus, while others provide a specified amount for each week of vacation taken.

*Industry pattern:* Vacation pay is computed on the basis of straight-time rates in 72 percent of non-manufacturing agreements, compared to 40 percent of manufacturing contracts. All other methods of computing vacation pay, inclusion of shift differentials, and vacation bonuses are found more often in manufacturing than in non-manufacturing agreements.

## Vacation Pay

*(Frequency Expressed as Percentage of Vacation Pay Provisions)*

|  | Based on Straight Time Rate | Based on Average Earnings | Either, Depending on Classification | Whichever is greater |
|---|---|---|---|---|
| All Industries | 50 | 33 | 8 | 8 |
| Manufacturing | 40 | 40 | 9 | 12 |
| Non-manufacturing | 72 | 20 | 8 | 1 |

Vacation pay is computed on regular rates in two-thirds or more of agreements in chemicals, communications, printing, transportation, and utilities. It is based on average earnings in more than two-thirds of contracts in primary metals and rubber. Vacation bonuses appear most frequently in electrical machinery, fabricated metals, machinery, primary metals, and transportation equipment.

## Work Requirements

To ensure that vacations are granted principally to employees who work a substantial portion of the year, many contracts condition vacation entitlement on a requirement that employees work a minimum time or percentage of available hours during the year. Fifty-three percent of all sample contracts contain a work requirement provision. These requirements are stated as a minimum number or amount of hours, days, weeks, months, or pay.

Less than one-half of a year is required in 18 percent of these provisions, one-half to three-quarters of a year is required in 53 percent, and more than three-quarters of a year is required in 29 percent. Of these requirements, 62 percent call for proration of vacation or vacation pay if the minimum work requirement is not met.

*Industry pattern:* Work requirements appear in 62 percent of manufacturing contracts and 38 percent of non-manufacturing agreements. Requirements usually are higher in non-manufacturing contracts, with 98 percent requiring one-half year or more, compared to 76 percent in manufacturing agreements.

More than two-thirds of contracts in fabricated metals, foods, furniture, leather, lumber, machinery, and mining contain work requirements.

Among industries in which a majority of contracts contain such provisions, requirements are strictest in fabricated metals, petroleum, retail, services, and transportation and are less strict in electrical machinery, machinery, paper, primary metals, and transportation equipment.

*No reduction in full vacation entitlement* is imposed for time lost for a variety of reasons under 53 percent of sample contracts. Of these provisions, 53 percent state that no reductions are allowed for time lost because of any illness or disability, and 36 percent state that vacations will not be reduced for absences due to occupational illness or disability. Other absences that do not result in loss of vacation under these provisions are military leave (32 percent), union leave (21 percent), jury duty and layoff (each 17 percent), funeral leave (8 percent), and other leaves or absences (15 percent).

*Industry pattern:* Provisions prohibiting a reduction in vacation for time lost due to specified absences are more prevalent in manufacturing (62 percent) than non-manufacturing (38 percent). They appear in a majority of contracts in 13 industries—chemicals, fabricated metals, foods, furniture, leather, lumber, machinery, mining, paper, primary metals, retail, transportation, and transportation equipment.

## Work During Vacation

More than half of the sample contracts studied consider the subject of work during vacations. Eleven percent of the agreements prohibit work during vacations, while 46 percent make some provision for work.

Of contracts allowing work, 98 percent impose some conditions. The employer may require work under 27 percent of these clauses, while employee consent is required under 36 percent, and union consent is required under 12 percent. Of these provisions, 10 percent specify that work will only be allowed in an emergency, and 32 percent limit work during only part of the vacation.

More than three-quarters of these clauses grant employees who work during their vacation vacation pay plus earnings, 11 percent allow employees to take a vacation on an alternate date, and 12 percent call for either method of compensation.

*Industry pattern:* Clauses prohibiting work during vacation appear in 9 percent of manufacturing and 14 percent of non-manufacturing agreements. Provisions allowing work during vacation are found in 58 percent of manufacturing contracts and in only 25 percent of non-manufacturing agreements. Under these clauses, employers may require work during vacation with about equal frequency in manufacturing (27 percent) and non-manufacturing (29 percent) agreements. Provisions requiring employee or union consent, however, are more common in non-manufacturing (66 percent) than in manufacturing (43 percent) contracts that permit work during vacation. Work is limited to only part of a vacation under 36 percent of the manufacturing provisions, compared to 16 percent of the non-manufacturing provisions. Employees are allowed to take a vacation on an alternate date in 16 percent of non-manufacturing provisions, compared to 9 percent of manufacturing.

## Vacation Scheduling

Vacation scheduling is mentioned in 87 percent of contracts analyzed. Forty-nine percent of these clauses call for plant or company shutdowns — either as a scheduled annual occurrence or an employer option. Thirteen percent of these provisions allow employees to select their vacations on the basis of seniority; 62 percent call for the employer to schedule vacations, giving consideration to employee choice and seniority; and 17 percent simply state that the employer will consider individual employee preferences. Vacation scheduling is a management prerogative under 5 percent of the vacation scheduling provisions.

*Industry pattern:* Plantwide vacation shutdowns are far more prevelant in manufacturing scheduling provisions (68 percent) than in non-manufacturing (8 percent). Industries in which a majority of contracts mention the possibility of shutdowns are electrical machinery, fabricated metals, furniture, leather, lumber, machinery, mining, paper, primary metals, rubber, stone-clay-glass, textiles, and transportation equipment.

Provisions giving management the prerogative to schedule vacations or those stipulating management will consider an employee's choice appear more frequently in manufacturing (90 percent) than in non-manufacturing (69 percent). Employee selection of vacation periods is much more common in non-manufacturing (29 percent) than in manufacturing (6 percent).

Vacation splitting is treated in 47 percent of the sample. Of these provisions, 4 percent require vacation splitting; 46 percent leave the choice to an employee; 10 percent leave the option with the employer; 35 percent call for mutual agreement.

Provisions for split vacations appear somewhat more frequently in manufacturing (49 percent) than in non-manufacturing (44 percent) agreements. The option of scheduling split vacations rests with the employer most frequently in manufacturing contracts, and with the employee most frequently in non-manufacturing agreements. Mutual agreement clauses appear in 39 percent of manufacturing and 29 percent of non-manufacturing industries.

**Cumulation of vacations** is mentioned in 50 percent of sample contracts. Cumulation from one year to the next is prohibited under 75 percent of these provisions, while 19 percent allow limited carry-over, and 7 percent allow full carry-over. Cumulation is prohibited in 79 percent of the provisions in manufacturing agreements and in 66 percent of the provisions in non-manufacturing agreements.

## Vacation Rights Upon Separation _____

Vacation entitlement for employees leaving a company's service is discussed in 79 percent of contracts in the database. Of these provisions, 52 percent grant pro-rata pay for time elapsed since the most recent vacation period, 30 percent grant vacation pay only if a vacation has been fully earned, and 19 percent grant pay based on one method or the other depending on the reason for termination.

### Vacation Rights Upon Separation

*(Frequency Expressed as Percentage of Separation Provisions)*

| Vacation pay granted upon: | All Industries | Manu-facturing | Non-manu-facturing |
|---|---|---|---|
| Death | 45 | 56 | 26 |
| Retirement | 44 | 55 | 24 |
| Layoff | 40 | 44 | 31 |
| Quit | 36 | 34 | 39 |
| Military Leave | 26 | 33 | 14 |
| Discharge | 29 | 27 | 33 |
| Separation for any reason | 18 | 20 | 13 |
| Any separation except discharge for cause or quit without notice | 9 | 4 | 19 |

# 16

# Wages

Provision for general wage increases, although of prime importance at the bargaining table, is not necessarily included in contracts. Cost-of-living adjustments and deferred increases continue to appear in agreements but show a decline in frequency since the 1983 study.

A new trend has emerged since the last analysis—provision for lump-sum payments in lieu of general wage increases. Two-tier systems, launched in 1983 in the aerospace industry, were first tracked in the last study.

## Long-Term Trends In Wage Negotiations

*(Frequency Expressed as Percentage of Contracts)*

|  | 1948 | 1950 | 1954 | 1957 | 1961 | 1966 | 1971 | 1975 | 1979 | 1983 | 1986 | 1989 |
|---|---|---|---|---|---|---|---|---|---|---|---|---|
| Deferred increases | — | — | 20 | 33 | 58 | 72 | 87 | 88 | 95 | 94 | 80 | 77 |
| Cost-of-living adjustments | — | — | 25 | 18 | 24 | 15 | 22 | 36 | 48 | 48 | 42 | 26 |
| Wage reopeners | 40 | 60 | 60 | 36 | 28 | 13 | 12 | 8 | 8 | 7 | 10 | 9 |

—Not tabulated until trend emerged.

Geographic analysis of the basic pattern database shows all contracts in New England provide for deferred increases, compared with about half of agreements in the Southwest and Rocky Mountain regions. Cost-of-living clauses and lump-sum payments appeared mainly in multiregion contracts and most wage reopeners were found in agreements in the Southeast and Southwest regions.

## Provisions For Wage Adjustment

*(Frequency Expressed as Percentage of Contracts in Each Region)*

|  | Deferred Increases | Active Cost-of-Living Escalators | Lump-Sum Payments | Reopeners |
|---|---|---|---|---|
| All REGIONS | 77 | 26 | 22 | 9 |
| Middle Atlantic | 84 | 23 | 17 | 6 |
| Midwest | 92 | 29 | 13 | 8 |
| New England | 100 | 24 | 16 | 4 |
| North Central | 75 | 27 | 20 | 2 |
| Rocky Mountain | 50 | 20 | 20 | — |
| Southeast | 76 | 12 | 22 | 22 |
| Southwest | 54 | 8 | 8 | 31 |
| West Coast | 80 | 28 | 26 | 7 |
| Multiregion | 58 | 48 | 35 | 8 |

Other employee compensation provisions commonly mentioned in contracts include supplementary pay (shift differentials, reporting and call-back or call-in pay, temporary transfer pay, hazardous duty pay, and job-related expenses) and establishment of pay rates (incentive pay, time study, and job classification). In addition, some agreements specify hiring and individual wage progression rates.

## Deferred Wage Increases

Deferred increases, such as annual improvement factors and productivity increases, are called for in 77 percent of the sample—down from 80 percent in the 1986 study and 94 percent in the 1983 analysis. The six-year drop is due in large part to steep declines in deferred increases in three industries (each with a 100 percent rate in the 1983 study): mining, 42 percent; primary metals, 36 percent; and transportation equipment, 59 percent.

Seventy-seven percent of deferred increases become effective at the beginning of the second year or, if more than one is provided, at yearly intervals. Five percent of deferred increases are paid semi-annually; 18 percent are paid quarterly or at widely varying intervals. Deferred increases are provided for in all sample contracts in the apparel, electrical machinery, printing, stone-clay-glass, and utilities industries. At least 85 percent of agreements in chemicals, communications, lumber, maritime, paper, petroleum, retail, and services call for deferred increases.

## Lump-Sum Payments

Lump-sum payments, other than Christmas and year-end bonuses, are found in 22 percent of contracts in the database—25 percent in manufacturing and 16 percent in non-manufacturing. Eighteen percent of the database provides for first-year payments, including ratification bonuses; 14 percent defer lump sums to later years.

*Industry pattern:* Lump-sum payments are found most frequently in transportation equipment (41 percent). Industries with a 29 percent to 33 percent frequency of such payments are chemicals, communications, electrical machinery, fabricated metals, foods, furniture, insurance and finance, petroleum, retail, and stone-clay-glass. None were found in construction and rubber sample contracts.

## Cost-Of-Living Provisions

The frequency of cost-of-living provisions has declined from a peak of 48 percent of contracts in the 1983 and the 1979 Basic Patterns surveys to 35 percent in the 1989 analysis. COLAs are more common in manufacturing (43 percent) than in non-manufacturing (21 percent) agreements.

Twenty-five percent of the provisions freeze any adjustments that might be generated by the c-o-l formula, leaving only 26 percent of sample contracts with active clauses. Active c-o-l clauses appear in 33 percent of manufacturing contracts and in 15 percent of non-manufacturing. Because details of frozen c-o-l provisions often do not appear in contracts, analysis of formulas is based on active clauses.

All but one of the 104 contracts containing active provisions tie adjustments to changes in the Bureau of Labor Statistics' Consumer Price Index. The one exception (in the transportation industry) uses the BLS Employment Cost Index. Eighty-nine percent of escalator provisions studied use the national All-Cities CPI as a base; 10 percent use selected city indexes.

Sixty-nine percent of active provisions call for adjustments of one cent for each specified percentage-point rise or change in CPI. The most frequently specified CPI movement is a 0.3 percentage point (38 percent of this type of formula), followed by 0.4 (26 percent). Adjustments based on the percentage CPI rise occur in 31 percent of active clauses.

Adjustments made at quarterly intervals appear predominately (70 percent) in manufacturing provisions; while annual adjustments are found in 12 percent. The reverse is true in the non-manufacturing sector where 74 percent of clauses call for annual COLAs and 17 percent for quarterly adjustments.

A limitation is placed on the amount of a c-o-l increase in 25 percent of the clauses analyzed. On an annual basis the most common ceiling or cap found in provisions with limits is 10 cents per hour (15 percent) followed by 25 cents (12 percent). The remainder range from maximum annual increases of 5 cents to 50 cents.

Under 33 percent of the c-o-l clauses, increases are paid only if CPI rises to a predetermined level. Any increase then granted is tied to the rise beyond such specified point.

Minimum adjustments, regardless of the rise in CPI, are guaranteed in 10 percent of active c-o-l clauses. Some contracts "float" accumulating COLAs above the base rate to prevent any affect on benefits tied to wages. Part or all of a float is folded or rolled into base rates at least once during contract term under 33 percent of active c-o-l clauses. Roll-ins generally occur at the beginning of a contract or annually.

Wage reductions in the event of a CPI decline are prohibited in 7 percent of active c-o-l provisions. A variation limiting the reduction—usually to the level of base wages at the beginning of the contract—is found in 28 percent of these clauses.

*Industry pattern:* Active c-o-l clauses are found in at least half of contracts in transportation equipment (71 percent), apparel (67 percent), fabricated metals (53 percent), and communications (50 percent). Freezes occurred most frequently in furniture (33 percent), followed closely by primary metals (32 percent). No leather, lumber, paper, petroleum, or utilities industry sample contracts contain COLA provisions.

## Wage Reopeners

Wage-reopening provisions allowing renegotiation of wages during the contract term are found in 9 percent of the sample. Such clauses are found in

6 percent of manufacturing agreements and in 12 percent of non-manufacturing agreements.

## Wage Structures

Two-tier wage systems set rates of new hires below those of employees already on the payroll. Tabulated in this section are lower rates that continue beyond the first six months of service. Twenty-eight percent of contracts in the database contain two-tier wage plans—a steep climb from 17 percent in the prior survey. Under 60 percent of these provisions, rates for new hires eventually catch up with those of more senior workers. Thirty-five percent of the two-tier systems permanently lower pay for new hires. Five percent lay out a mixed system such as permanent two-tier rates for lower grades and temporary two-tier rates for higher grades.

*Industry pattern:* More than one-half of sample contracts in the following industries provide for two-tier wages: foods (67 percent), fabricated metals (58 percent), and retail and transportation (each 52 percent). None of these provisions were found in apparel, communications, construction, leather, and lumber.

*Hiring rates* set lower than standard rates for up to six months are specified in 10 percent of sample contracts—14 percent in manufacturing and 5 percent in non-manufacturing. Such provisions stipulate that newly hired employees automatically advance to the regular job rate after a specified period of time.

While under these clauses hiring rates range from 5 cents to $5.18 below standard hourly rates, 10-cent, 15-cent, and $1.00 differentials are the most common (each 14 percent), followed by 50 cents, 60 cents, and $1.20 (each 10 percent).

Time periods required to reach the standard rate vary from 20 days to six months. The most common period specified in these clauses is 180 days (22 percent), followed by 90 days (14 percent), and 30 days and 120 days (each 11 percent).

*Wage progression* systems specifying rate ranges rather than single rates appear in 44 percent of contracts—42 percent in manufacturing and 47 percent in non-manufacturing. Progression from minimum to higher rates in a range may be based on length of service (72 percent of such systems), or may be affected by merit (28 percent).

Periodic review of employees' progress to determine eligibility for progression to the next step in the range is required in 15 percent of wage progression provisions.

## Supplementary Pay

Extra pay for late shifts is required in 85 percent of contracts surveyed—93 percent in manufacturing and 74 percent in non-manufacturing.

The absence of shift premiums in most of the remaining contracts simply reflects a lack of late-shift work.

Shift-differentials are flat cents per hour payments in 75 percent of contracts with one night shift, 72 percent of second-shift premiums and 67 percent of third-shift premiums. In the remainder of these clauses, premiums are a percentage of the base rate, vary from job to job, or offer the same pay for fewer hours.

Larger premiums are paid for third shifts than for second shifts in 84 percent of contracts that schedule second and third shifts; the same premiums are paid for both second and third shifts in the remaining 16 percent.

Median cents-per-hour premiums are 25 cents for contracts with one night shift, 25 cents for second shifts, and 30 cents for third shifts. Median percentage premiums are 9 percent (of the base rate) for second shifts and 10 percent each for third shifts and night shifts.

### Second-Shift Differentials

| | Cents Per Hour[1] | | | | | | Percentage of Hourly Pay[2] | | | | | |
|---|---|---|---|---|---|---|---|---|---|---|---|---|
| | 1-10¢ | 11-20¢ | 21-30¢ | 31-40¢ | 41-50¢ | Over 50¢ | 1-3% | 4-6% | 7-9% | 10-12% | 13-15% | Over 15% |
| All Industries | 8 | 36 | 30 | 10 | 12 | 4 | 7 | 36 | 7 | 41 | 2 | 7 |
| Manufacturing | 7 | 40 | 32 | 10 | 10 | 1 | 9 | 34 | 6 | 47 | — | 3 |
| Non-manufacturing | 11 | 26 | 26 | 9 | 17 | 13 | — | 42 | 8 | 25 | 8 | 17 |

[1]Frequency expressed as percentage of contracts calling for cents-per-hour second-shift differentials.
[2]Frequency expressed as percentage of contracts calling for second-shift differentials based on a percentage of hourly pay.

### Third-Shift Differentials

| | Cents Per Hour[1] | | | | | | Percentage of Hourly Pay[2] | | | | | |
|---|---|---|---|---|---|---|---|---|---|---|---|---|
| | 20¢ and under | 21-30¢ | 31-40¢ | 41-50¢ | 51-60¢ | Over 60¢ | 1-3% | 4-6% | 7-9% | 10-12% | 13-15% | Over 15% |
| All Industries | 21 | 30 | 19 | 13 | 9 | 9 | — | 14 | 14 | 50 | 14 | 8 |
| Manufacturing | 23 | 34 | 18 | 10 | 7 | 7 | — | 17 | 13 | 58 | 8 | 4 |
| Non-manufacturing | 13 | 17 | 20 | 24 | 13 | 13 | — | 8 | 17 | 33 | 25 | 17 |

[1]Frequency expressed as percentage of contracts calling for cents-per-hour third-shift differentials.
[2]Frequency expressed as percentage of contracts calling for third-shift differentials based on a percentage of hourly pay.

## Night-Shift Differentials

| | Cents Per Hour[1] | | | | | | Percentage of Hourly Pay[2] | | | | | |
|---|---|---|---|---|---|---|---|---|---|---|---|---|
| | 1-10¢ | 11-20¢ | 21-30¢ | 31-40¢ | 41-50¢ | Over 50¢ | 1-3% | 4-6% | 7-9% | 10-12% | 13-15% | Over 15% |
| All Industries | 22 | 22 | 24 | 8 | 10 | 14 | — | 7 | — | 80 | 7 | 7 |
| Manufacturing | 31 | 31 | 19 | 4 | 4 | 12 | — | — | — | 100 | — | — |
| Non-manufacturing | 13 | 13 | 29 | 13 | 17 | 17 | — | 17 | — | 50 | 17 | 17 |

[1]Frequency expressed as percentage of contracts calling for cents-per-hour night-shift differentials.
[2]Frequency expressed as percentage of contracts calling for night-shift differentials based on a percentage of hourly pay.

*Industry pattern:* All sample contracts in the following industries provide for shift differentials: chemicals, communications, electrical machinery, fabricated metals, lumber, paper, rubber, transportation equipment, and utilities. At least 85 percent of agreements in construction, foods, machinery, mining, petroleum, primary metals, stone-clay-glass, and textiles include these provisions.

**Reporting pay** for employees who report for work as scheduled but find no work available is guaranteed in 78 percent of the contracts. The prevalence of reporting-pay provisions is much greater in manufacturing (91 percent) than in non-manufacturing (58 percent).

The guarantee is inapplicable under 68 percent of the reporting-pay provisions if work is unavailable for reasons beyond the company's control, and under 31 percent if an employee refuses work that is available.

The amount of reporting pay guaranteed varies from one to eight hours. Of contracts containing reporting-pay guarantees, 65 percent guarantee four hours of pay; 14 percent, two hours; and 13 percent, eight hours. Under 11 percent of these provisions the guarantee is increased if an employee actually begins work.

## Reporting Pay

*(Frequency Expressed as Percentage of Reporting Pay Provisions)*

| | Guaranteed Hours | | | | | | | |
|---|---|---|---|---|---|---|---|---|
| | 1 | 2 | 3 | 4 | 5 | 6 | 7 | 8 |
| All Industries | 2 | 14 | 5 | 65 | — | 1 | 1 | 13 |
| Manufacturing | — | 7 | 6 | 77 | — | 1 | 1 | 8 |
| Non-manufacturing | 6 | 33 | 2 | 33 | — | 1 | — | 25 |

*Industry pattern:* Reporting pay appears in all contracts in the furniture, leather, lumber, mining, paper, primary metals, rubber, and textiles industries, and in at least 85 percent of agreements in apparel, chemicals, construction, electrical machinery, fabricated metals, machinery, petroleum, stone-clay-glass, and transportation equipment.

*Call-back or call-in pay,* to cover situations in which employees are called in or back to work at some time other than their regularly scheduled hours, is guaranteed in 67 percent of the sample—76 percent in manufacturing and 53 percent in non-manufacturing.

Amount of call-back or call-in pay guaranteed varies from two hours to eight hours. Guarantees most frequently are four hours (63 percent of the provisions), followed by two hours (19 percent), and three hours (12 percent). In only 3 percent of these provisions are the guarantees increased if an employee actually begins work.

Premium rates are guaranteed in 33 percent of call-back or call-in clauses, with 12 percent paying premiums only for hours actually worked.

Under 8 percent of call-back or call-in clauses employees may quit work as soon as the required work is accomplished, even though the full guarantee-time has not been worked and other work is available. Seven percent of the provisions specify that other work may be assigned until guarantee time has elapsed, and 12 percent invalidate the guarantee if work is prevented due to causes beyond control by the company.

### Call-Back, Call-In Pay

*(Frequency Expressed as Percentage of Call-Back, Call-In Provisions)*

|  | Guaranteed Hours | | | | | | | |
|---|---|---|---|---|---|---|---|---|
|  | 1 | 2 | 3 | 4 | 5 | 6 | 7 | 8 |
| All Industries | — | 19 | 12 | 63 | 1 | 2 | — | 4 |
| Manufacturing | — | 14 | 10 | 71 | 1 | 2 | — | 3 |
| Non-manufacturing | — | 31 | 17 | 44 | — | 3 | — | 5 |

*Industry pattern:* All sample contracts in the chemicals, mining, petroleum, and utilities industries contain call-in or call-back guarantees, while 85 percent or more of those in the communications, electrical machinery, fabricated metals, machinery, paper, and transportation equipment industries call for guarantees.

*Pay for temporary transfer* is provided in 64 percent of sample agreements—74 percent in manufacturing and 48 percent in non-manufacturing. Transfer to a higher-rated job is covered in 61 percent of contracts; transfer to a lower-rated job in 52 percent.

Transfer to a higher-rated job clauses most frequently (72 percent) state that the higher rate will be paid immediately. Twenty-six percent of these grant the higher rate but exclude temporary transfers of short duration and 3 percent specify that the old rate be retained.

Of contracts providing for transfer to a lower-rated job, 95 percent specify retention of the old rate. Immediate rate cuts are stipulated in 2 percent of these provisions; cuts after a time lag are called for in 3 percent.

*Hazardous work premiums* are provided for in 12 percent of the sample. These premiums are found in the following industries—chemicals, communications, construction, foods, machinery, maritime, mining, petroleum, retail, rubber, services, transportation, transportation equipment, and utilities. Premiums for "dirty work" appear in 5 percent of contracts studied and are found in seven industries—chemicals, construction, machinery, maritime, transportation, transportation equipment, and utilities.

*Travel expenses* necessitated by the job are considered in 31 percent of contracts in the database—55 percent in non-manufacturing and 16 percent in manufacturing. Many agreements contain several types of expense-reimbursement provisions, falling in the categories listed below:

(1) Expenses when away from headquarters—55 percent of travel expense provisions—found primarily in communications, construction, fabricated metals, maritime, petroleum, transportation, transportation equipment, and utilities.

(2) Mileage rate for use of own car when on company business—40 percent of such provisions—appearing mainly in communications, construction, maritime, retail, and utilities.

(3) Daily allowances for travel—34 percent of travel expense provisions—concentrated in communications, construction, maritime, transportation, and utilities.

(4) Moving and transfer expenses—36 percent of expense provisions—found most frequently in communications, primary metals, transportation, transportation equipment, and utilities.

## Travel Expenses

*(Frequency Expressed as Percentage of Contracts\*)*

| | Car Mileage | Expenses Away from Home Office | Flat Daily Travel Allowance | Moving and Transfer |
|---|---|---|---|---|
| All Industries | 13 | 17 | 11 | 11 |
| Manufacturing | 3 | 9 | 3 | 9 |
| Non-manufacturing | 27 | 31 | 23 | 16 |

*Many contracts contain more than one type.

*Work clothes* required by the job, not including safety clothes and equipment (see Chapter 17), are considered in 33 percent of contracts surveyed. Such provisions appear in 19 percent of manufacturing contracts and in 56 percent of non-manufacturing agreements. Work clothes provisions most often appear in transportation (76 percent), retail and services (each 74 percent), utilities (70 percent), chemicals (63 percent), foods (57 percent), construction (41 percent), and communications (40 percent).

Employers are required to supply work clothes in 71 percent of contracts that discuss the subject. This requirement prevails in retail (74 percent), services (70 percent), transportation (68 percent), and chemicals (56 percent).

The cost of laundering or replacing work clothes is borne by employers in 51 percent of these provisions.

**Tools** required on the job are discussed in 25 percent of contracts (17 percent in manufacturing and 37 percent in non-manufacturing). Employers supply the tools in 73 percent of such provisions and furnish replacements in 50 percent.

**Bonuses,** other than direct production bonuses, are provided in 8 percent of agreements studied. While there is little concentration on any particular type of bonus, Christmas and year-end bonuses are typical.

## Establishment of Wage Rates

*Incentive or piecework pay* is discussed in one-third of contracts analyzed. Six percent of the agreements either prohibit establishment of an incentive plan or require union consent to adopt a plan. Incentive provisions appear in 49 percent of manufacturing agreements and in only 8 percent of non-manufacturing contracts. Implementation of incentives is barred or restricted in 7 percent of manufacturing agreements and in 6 percent of non-manufacturing contracts.

Most agreements that mention incentive operations do not elaborate on details of the system. Typical provisions primarily concern the union's role in setting or protesting standards, safeguards against speedups or rate cutting, and rules for conducting time studies.

Of contracts discussing establishment of new incentive rates or production standards during the contract term (24 percent of the sample), 66 percent permit the company to establish new rates without union participation, 23 percent call for consultation with the union, and 11 percent require union consent.

Limitations on rate revision are imposed in 68 percent of contracts containing systems incentive. Sixty-four percent of limiting clauses state that rates shall be changed only when an element (such as method, material, equipment, or product) of the job changes. Thirty percent specify that the change be substantial. Thirty-seven percent of limiting provisions allow revision when an existing rate is in error; many permit changes for more than one reason.

*Industry pattern:* Incentive provisions are found in all sample contracts in apparel. Other industries in which more than half of the agreements mention incentives are electrical machinery, fabricated metals, furniture, leather, machinery, primary metals, rubber, stone-clay-glass, and textiles. Such clauses are nonexistent in the petroleum and printing industries, and are rare in the non-manufacturing sector (if sales commission arrangements are not considered).

***Time-study plans*** are found in 34 percent of manufacturing contracts and in only one non-manufacturing (retail industry) contract.

Contracts may include one or more of the following typical conditions contained in time-study provisions:

(1) Observation by a union representative allowed during a time study (4 percent).

(2) Special training provided for union time-study representatives (15 percent).

(3) Availability of time-study records to employees or union required (24 percent).

(4) Availability of records required only in case of dispute (16 percent).

(5) Timing limited to an "average" or "normal" employee (51 percent).

(6) Notice to employee and/or union when a job is being timed (34 percent).

(7) Requirement that fatigue and personal allowances be built into rate (41 percent).

Special procedures for handling time-study disputes (other than the grievance procedure) are included in 54 percent of time-study clauses. Joint re-examination by union and management is called for in 60 percent of the procedures; by the company alone, in 16 percent. Unions are permitted to check the study under 18 percent of the procedures. Seven percent of these clauses require that time-study disputes be heard by an arbiter specially qualified to deal with such disagreements (usually a trained industrial engineer).

Disputes are subject to grievance procedures and/or arbitration in 43 percent of time-study clauses.

*Industry pattern:* At least half of the contracts in the following industries contain time-study procedures: electrical machinery, furniture, leather, machinery, rubber, stone-clay-glass, and textiles. A third or more of fabricated metals and transportation equipment agreements include these procedures. Such clauses are nonexistent in apparel, petroleum, and printing, and in all non-manufacturing industry agreements except the one in retail.

***Job classification procedures*** for changing or establishing new categories during the contract term are spelled out in 58 percent of the sample—69 percent in manufacturing and 41 percent in non-manufacturing.

Of agreements containing job classification procedures, 44 percent require union consultation or notification before a classification may be changed or established; 36 percent require the company to negotiate with the union. Job classification is considered a management prerogative under 9 percent of classification procedures and is subject to review by a joint labor-management committee under 9 percent.

Disputes are subject to grievance procedures in 54 percent of the provisions. Arbitration is called for under 43 percent of the clauses.

## Wage Provisions By Industry

*(Frequency Expressed as Percentage of Industry Contracts)*

| | Deferred Increase | Active Cost-of-Living | Lump Sums | Wage Reopening | Two-Tier System | Wage Progression | Reporting Pay | Call-Back, Call-in | Temporary Transfer | Wage Incentive | Job Classification | Shift Differential | Hazard/Dirty Pay | Travel Expenses | Work Clothes | Tools |
|---|---|---|---|---|---|---|---|---|---|---|---|---|---|---|---|---|
| ALL INDUSTRIES | 77 | 26 | 22 | 9 | 28 | 44 | 78 | 67 | 64 | 33 | 58 | 85 | 13 | 31 | 33 | 25 |
| MANUFACTURING | 75 | 33 | 25 | 6 | 29 | 42 | 91 | 76 | 74 | 49 | 69 | 93 | 7 | 16 | 19 | 17 |
| Apparel | 100 | 67 | 11 | — | — | 22 | 89 | — | 67 | 100 | — | 22 | — | — | — | 44 |
| Chemicals | 94 | 13 | 31 | — | 25 | 56 | 88 | 100 | 88 | 25 | 75 | 100 | 19 | 6 | 63 | 25 |
| Electrical Machinery | 100 | 35 | 30 | 5 | 35 | 80 | 90 | 90 | 70 | 65 | 85 | 100 | — | 10 | 10 | 15 |
| Fabricated Metals | 79 | 53 | 32 | — | 58 | 42 | 95 | 89 | 89 | 63 | 74 | 100 | — | 21 | 11 | 5 |
| Foods | 76 | 19 | 33 | 10 | 67 | 24 | 81 | 81 | 76 | 19 | 62 | 95 | 10 | 29 | 57 | 33 |
| Furniture | 83 | 33 | 33 | — | 17 | 17 | 100 | 83 | 67 | 67 | 67 | 67 | — | — | 17 | 17 |
| Leather | 75 | — | 25 | — | — | 100 | 100 | — | 75 | 75 | 50 | 75 | — | — | — | 25 |
| Lumber | 86 | — | 14 | 14 | — | — | 100 | 71 | 86 | 14 | 86 | 100 | — | — | 29 | 14 |
| Machinery | 69 | 38 | 23 | 4 | 19 | 85 | 92 | 85 | 85 | 62 | 81 | 96 | 8 | 8 | 23 | 4 |
| Paper | 93 | — | 14 | — | 29 | 14 | 100 | 93 | 93 | 14 | 86 | 100 | — | 7 | 7 | 21 |
| Petroleum | 86 | — | 29 | — | 29 | 14 | 86 | 100 | 86 | — | 57 | 86 | 14 | 29 | 14 | 43 |
| Primary Metals | 36 | 32 | 12 | 4 | 16 | 24 | 100 | 56 | 68 | 64 | 72 | 96 | — | 24 | 8 | 8 |
| Printing | 100 | 25 | 13 | 13 | 13 | 13 | 25 | 75 | 50 | — | 38 | 75 | — | 13 | 13 | 13 |
| Rubber | 50 | 33 | — | 33 | 17 | — | 100 | 50 | 67 | 83 | 50 | 100 | 17 | — | 17 | — |
| Stone-Clay-Glass | 100 | 31 | 31 | — | 8 | 23 | 85 | 62 | 69 | 69 | 69 | 92 | — | — | 15 | 23 |
| Textiles | 50 | — | 10 | 60 | 10 | 40 | 100 | 50 | 80 | 70 | 60 | 90 | — | — | 10 | — |
| Transportation Equipment | 59 | 71 | 41 | — | 41 | 59 | 97 | 88 | 53 | 41 | 71 | 100 | 24 | 44 | 6 | 21 |
| NON-MANUFACTURING | 80 | 15 | 16 | 12 | 28 | 47 | 58 | 53 | 48 | 8 | 41 | 74 | 23 | 55 | 56 | 37 |
| Communications | 90 | 50 | 30 | 10 | — | 100 | 30 | 90 | 100 | — | 70 | 100 | 10 | 100 | 40 | 30 |
| Construction | 76 | 3 | — | 14 | — | 3 | 93 | 21 | 24 | 3 | 17 | 97 | 48 | 66 | 41 | 69 |
| Insurance & Finance | 71 | 14 | 29 | — | 14 | 71 | — | 29 | 43 | 14 | 57 | 57 | — | 14 | — | — |
| Maritime | 88 | 38 | 13 | 25 | 38 | 25 | 25 | 38 | 25 | — | 13 | 25 | 63 | 75 | 38 | 13 |
| Mining | 42 | 17 | 17 | 17 | 8 | 8 | 100 | 100 | 100 | 42 | 75 | 92 | 33 | 17 | 8 | 67 |
| Retail | 85 | 15 | 30 | 4 | 52 | 56 | 52 | 33 | 26 | 11 | 48 | 63 | 4 | 41 | 74 | 33 |
| Services | 96 | 7 | 15 | 19 | 33 | 48 | 56 | 56 | 37 | 7 | 48 | 59 | 4 | 30 | 74 | 4 |
| Transportation | 68 | 20 | 12 | — | 52 | 68 | 56 | 64 | 52 | — | 24 | 64 | 24 | 76 | 76 | 48 |
| Utilities | 100 | — | 10 | 40 | 20 | 80 | 30 | 100 | 100 | 10 | 50 | 100 | 40 | 90 | 70 | 30 |

*Industry pattern:* Job classification clauses are found in at least three-quarters of agreements in six industries: lumber and paper (each 86 percent), electrical machinery (85 percent), machinery (81 percent), and chemicals and mining (each 75 percent).

---

# 17

# Working Conditions: Safety and Health; Discrimination

Provisions expressing an individual employee's interest in broad areas beyond the contractual protection of wages, jobs, and benefits are included in most union agreements. Occupational safety and health and non-discrimination, for example, were each dealt with in at least 86 percent of agreements contained in the Basic Patterns database.

## Occupational Safety and Health

Occupational safety and health clauses are found in 86 percent of the 400 sample agreements. Geographic analysis shows that such provisions are included in from 79 to 92 percent of contracts in areas designated in the database.

Safety-health clauses vary considerably. Some contracts merely contain a general statement of responsibility for the safety and health of employees, while others go into detail and consider such issues as safety equipment, first aid, physical examinations, investigation of accidents, employee obligations, hazardous work, safety committees, and substance abuse.

*Industry pattern:* Safety and health clauses are included in 94 percent of manufacturing agreements and 74 percent of non-manufacturing contracts. These provisions appear in all rubber, mining, leather, primary metals, fabricated metals, petroleum, textiles, paper, printing, and maritime contracts. At least 80 percent of agreements in all other industries except communications (70 percent), apparel (67 percent), services (59 percent), retail (56 percent), and insurance and finance (29 percent) contain safety and health provisions.

Of contracts with safety and health clauses, 38 percent include a statement that the company will comply with federal, state, and/or local laws, and 68 percent include a general statement of responsibility for employees' safety and health. Forty-seven percent of the general statements apply to both management and union; the remainder apply only to the employer.

Safety equipment, such as guards and shields around machinery and safety boots and goggles to be worn by employees, is mentioned in 43 percent of the sample contracts. Of these provisions, 65 percent specify that the company will furnish all safety equipment at no cost to employees, and 10 percent state that employees will share some of the cost (often for replacements only) of wearing apparel.

*First aid supplies* and/or facilities are provided for in 22 percent of the contracts studied—25 percent in manufacturing and 17 percent in non-manufacturing. A requirement that a registered nurse be on duty, at least during the day shift, is found in 19 percent of first aid clauses. A stipulation that at least one employee or supervisor trained in first aid be present at all times also is included in 19 percent of these provisions.

*Physical examinations* are required in 33 percent of the sample. Of these clauses, 25 percent require physicals of new hires, 34 percent require physicals when employees are rehired or return to work from layoff or leave, and 63 percent require physicals periodically or at management's request. Employees may appeal an unfavorable opinion under 39 percent of the physical examination provisions.

## Safety and Health Provisions

*(Frequency Expressed as Percentage of Industry Contracts)*

| | Provisions | General Statement of Responsibility | Company to Comply with Laws | Safety Equipment | Company Provides First Aid | Physical Examinations | Accident Investigations | Hazardous Work Provisions | Safety Committees |
|---|---|---|---|---|---|---|---|---|---|
| ALL INDUSTRIES | 86 | 59 | 33 | 43 | 22 | 33 | 18 | 26 | 48 |
| MANUFACTURING | 94 | 68 | 33 | 49 | 25 | 34 | 24 | 26 | 62 |
| Apparel | 67 | 22 | 22 | — | — | 11 | — | — | 22 |
| Chemicals | 94 | 63 | 13 | 69 | 38 | 50 | 25 | 25 | 69 |
| Electrical Machinery | 80 | 50 | 40 | 35 | 20 | 15 | 15 | 10 | 40 |
| Fabricated Metals | 100 | 84 | 53 | 89 | 32 | 37 | 32 | 37 | 74 |
| Foods | 90 | 57 | 33 | 43 | 14 | 38 | 10 | 19 | 52 |
| Furniture | 83 | 67 | 17 | 33 | — | — | 17 | 33 | 33 |
| Leather | 100 | 50 | 25 | 25 | — | 25 | 25 | — | 75 |
| Lumber | 86 | 43 | 14 | 29 | 14 | — | — | — | 57 |
| Machinery | 92 | 81 | 27 | 62 | 12 | 31 | 23 | 19 | 69 |
| Paper | 100 | 71 | 14 | 29 | 36 | 21 | 14 | 14 | 43 |
| Petroleum | 100 | 29 | — | — | 14 | 100 | 86 | 29 | 86 |
| Primary Metals | 100 | 80 | 56 | 64 | 52 | 44 | 48 | 52 | 88 |
| Printing | 100 | 63 | 63 | — | 13 | — | — | — | — |
| Rubber | 100 | 100 | 83 | 83 | 50 | 83 | 67 | 17 | 100 |
| Stone-Clay-Glass | 92 | 38 | 15 | 54 | 15 | 38 | 8 | 31 | 62 |
| Textiles | 100 | 100 | 30 | 30 | 10 | 10 | — | 20 | 40 |
| Transportation Equipment | 97 | 85 | 29 | 59 | 32 | 47 | 32 | 44 | 82 |
| NON-MANUFACTURING | 74 | 44 | 33 | 34 | 17 | 30 | 9 | 26 | 26 |
| Communications | 70 | 40 | — | 26 | 10 | — | — | 20 | 50 |
| Construction | 86 | 41 | 66 | 59 | 14 | 3 | 10 | 31 | 7 |
| Insurance & Finance | 29 | 29 | 14 | — | — | — | — | — | — |
| Maritime | 100 | 75 | 50 | 75 | 50 | 63 | — | 63 | 50 |
| Mining | 100 | 92 | 58 | 100 | 42 | 75 | 50 | 67 | 83 |
| Retail | 56 | 26 | 22 | 4 | 22 | 30 | — | 15 | 4 |
| Services | 59 | 33 | 26 | 11 | 11 | 19 | 4 | 4 | 15 |
| Transportation | 88 | 36 | 24 | 28 | 12 | 72 | 4 | 32 | 36 |
| Utilities | 80 | 80 | 10 | 40 | — | — | 30 | 30 | 50 |

*Investigation of on-the-job accidents* are discussed in 18 percent of the sample contracts—24 percent in manufacturing and 9 percent in non-manufacturing. More than one-half (53 percent) of these provisions call for joint company-union investigation of accidents; 38 percent call for company investigations and require that the union be given reports; 8 percent call for company investigations and require that the union have access to the records.

*Employee obligations* in maintaining safety and health standards are stated in 40 percent of agreements included in the study. These provisions are found in 44 percent of manufacturing contracts and 32 percent of non-manufacturing contracts.

The most common requirement appearing in employee obligation provisions is obedience of all safety rules (65 percent). Other employee obligation clauses require that workers use safety equipment (38 percent), report all injuries (26 percent), and report any unsafe working conditions (18 percent). Disciplinary action is specified for violation of safety rules under 39 percent of contracts in which employee obligations are discussed.

*Industry pattern:* Employee obligations are specified in at least one-half of agreements in leather and chemicals (each 50 percent), fabricated metals (53 percent), stone-clay-glass (54 percent), mining and rubber (each 67 percent), and paper (86 percent). These provisions appear in at least one-quarter of contracts in all other industries with the exception of apparel, petroleum, communications, utilities, retail, and insurance and finance.

### Employee Obligations

*(Frequency Expressed as Percentage of Employee Obligation Provisions)*

|  | All Industries | Manufacturing | Non-manufacturing |
|---|---|---|---|
| Must Obey Safety Rules | 65 | 62 | 70 |
| Must Report All Injuries | 26 | 26 | 26 |
| Must Use Safety Equipment | 38 | 46 | 20 |
| Must Report Unsafe Working Conditions | 18 | 19 | 14 |
| Disciplinary Action for Violation of Rules | 39 | 38 | 42 |

*Joint company-union pledges* to encourage employees with substance abuse problems to seek rehabilitation are found in 36 (up from 27 in the 1986 study) of the 400 sample contracts—28 in manufacturing and 8 in non-manufacturing. Eleven of the agreements analyzed permit substance abuse testing.

## Hazardous Work

Provisions placing some type of restriction on employee performance of hazardous work are found in 26 percent of agreements contained in the database—26 percent in manufacturing and 26 percent in non-manufacturing. Of these clauses, 29 percent guarantee employees the right to refuse hazardous work, 58 percent state that employees are not required to engage in work they believe is unsafe, and 34 percent stipulate that employees may file a grievance if required to work under abnormally hazardous conditions. Only four of the 400 contracts grant rate retention rights during temporary transfers because of hazardous conditions or injuries, while seven contain "Right To Know" clauses which require employers to identify the presence of harmful or toxic substances.

## Safety and Health Committees

Joint management-union safety and health committees are called for in almost one-half (48 percent) of sample agreements. Periodic committee meetings are specified in 72 percent of contracts providing for such committees; periodic inspections of the plant in 46 percent. Pay for time spent on committee activities during regular work hours is stipulated in 39 percent of safety-health committee clauses. Issues left unresolved may be referred to a grievance and/or arbitration procedure under 30 percent of these provisions. Eleven percent of committee provisions state that the union's role in health-safety issues is strictly advisory and not subject to liability for any illness or injury.

### Safety and Health Committees

*(Frequency Expressed as Percentage of Committee Provisions)*

|  | All Industries | Manu-facturing | Non-manufacturing |
|---|---|---|---|
| Periodic Meetings | 72 | 74 | 65 |
| Periodic Inspections | 46 | 48 | 38 |
| Pay for Time Spent on Committee Activities | 39 | 41 | 35 |
| Disputed Issues Subject to Grievance & Arbitration | 30 | 28 | 40 |

## Inspections and Investigations

Inspections and investigations by government occupational safety and health officers are discussed in 12 percent of agreements analyzed. All of these provisions state that a union representative may accompany a safety-health inspector touring the premises; a majority (52 percent) specify pay for time spent in government investigations and inspections.

*Industry pattern:* Inspection and investigation by health and safety officers is mentioned in 50 percent each of rubber and mining contracts, and in at least 25 percent of fabricated metals, transportation equipment, leather, and chemicals contracts.

## Safety and Health Provisions

*(Frequency Expressed as Percentage of Contracts in Each Region)*

|  | Middle Atlantic | Midwest | New England | North Central | Rocky Mountain | Southeast | Southwest | West Coast | Multiregion |
|---|---|---|---|---|---|---|---|---|---|
| Provisions | 87 | 79 | 84 | 87 | 80 | 92 | 92 | 80 | 85 |
| General Statement of Responsibility | 52 | 46 | 60 | 69 | 60 | 74 | 46 | 50 | 53 |
| Company to Comply with Laws | 34 | 29 | 32 | 26 | 50 | 30 | 23 | 52 | 30 |
| Safety Equipment | 35 | 38 | 28 | 46 | 50 | 50 | 54 | 35 | 55 |
| Company Provides First Aid | 17 | 17 | 24 | 23 | — | 22 | 38 | 17 | 37 |
| Physical Examinations | 22 | 25 | 12 | 36 | 10 | 32 | 46 | 33 | 55 |
| Accident Investigation | 13 | 17 | 8 | 21 | 10 | 14 | 23 | 13 | 33 |
| Hazardous Work Provisions | 19 | 21 | 8 | 19 | 50 | 28 | 31 | 24 | 48 |
| Safety Committees | 33 | 29 | 24 | 42 | 10 | 32 | 23 | 30 | 47 |

## Guarantees Against Discrimination _____

Guarantees against discrimination—by either the union, the company, or both—appear in 94 percent of the sample. Geographic analysis reveals that non-discrimination provisions are found in from 80 to 97 percent of contracts in designated areas contained in the database.

Thirty percent of contracts containing non-discrimination clauses include a statement that any federal, state, and/or local laws prohibiting discrimination will be complied with.

***Discrimination on the basis of race, color, creed, sex, national origin, or age*** is banned in 87 percent of agreements analyzed. The majority of these provisions (93 percent) either apply the ban to both management and union or make no reference to either party. Only 7 percent of the non-discrimination clauses apply to management alone.

*Industry pattern:* Ninety-one percent of manufacturing agreements and 80 percent of non-manufacturing contracts contain provisions prohibiting discrimination on the basis of race, color, creed, sex, national origin, or age. Such clauses are found in from 80 to 100 percent of all sample contracts except those in transportation (68 percent), insurance and finance (71 percent), construction (72 percent), maritime and printing (each 75 percent), and services (78 percent).

***Discrimination because of union membership or non-membership*** is prohibited in 57 percent of the sample. The ban applies only to management in 44 percent of these provisions and only to the union in 4 percent. The remainder either apply the ban to both union and management or make no reference to either party.

*Industry pattern:* Discrimination because of union membership is prohibited in 56 percent of manufacturing agreements and 59 percent of non-manufacturing contracts. Such provisions are found in all contracts in petroleum, 86 percent in insurance and finance, 79 percent in fabricated metals, 70 percent each in electrical machinery, and communications, and in at least one-third of contracts in all other industries except apparel, printing, and rubber.

**Discrimination because of union activity** is barred in 39 percent of contracts surveyed. Of these provisions, 62 percent apply the ban only to management; the remainder either make a general statement or apply the ban to both parties.

*Industry pattern:* Discrimination because of union activity is prohibited in 34 percent of manufacturing agreements and in 46 percent of non-manufacturing contracts. These provisions appear in at least one-half of the agreements in insurance and finance (71 percent), communications (70 percent), retail (67 percent), and leather, electrical machinery, mining, and maritime (each 50 percent).

Bans against discrimination because of political activity or affiliation, marital status, mental or physical handicap, sexual preference or against Vietnam veterans have been introduced in agreements over the past few years and now are tabulated in the Basic Patterns analysis. Provisions prohibiting discrimination on the basis of one or more of the listed items appear in 40 percent of the sample, up from 30 percent in the 1986 study. Such clauses appear in 44 percent of manufacturing and 35 percent of non-manufacturing contracts.

**Equal employment opportunity pledges** appear in 17 percent of contracts studied. These pledges are found in 14 percent of manufacturing and 21 percent of non-manufacturing agreements. A majority (79 percent) of these provisions contain joint management-union pledges.

### Non-discrimination Provisions

*(Frequency Expressed as Percentage of Contracts)*

|  | All Industries | Manu-facturing | Non-manu-facturing |
|---|---|---|---|
| Provisions | 94 | 95 | 93 |
| No Discrimination on Basis of: |  |  |  |
| Race, Color, Creed, Sex, |  |  |  |
| National Origin, or Age | 87 | 91 | 80 |
| Union Membership or Nonmembership | 57 | 56 | 59 |
| Union Activity | 39 | 34 | 46 |
| Equal Employment Opportunity Pledges | 17 | 14 | 21 |

# Index